## THE AIR THAT KILLED

He walked to the batwings, shoved them open, and stepped to the boardwalk. He sniffed deeply of the fresh air to get the saloon out of his lungs, then froze in his tracks. From somewhere, carried on some vagrant breeze, had come a remembered smell, one that had become imprinted on his senses until there could be no mistake.

It was the rich smell of expensive tobacco, the same that had filled his nostrils the night he stood seething with impotent rage as he sniffed the cheroot butt dropped by the cold-blooded killer of a harmless old man . . .

# SADDLE TRAMP

JOHN L. SHELLEY

A BERKLEY MEDALLION BOOK
published by
BERKLEY PUBLISHING CORPORATION

*Published by arrangement with*
*the author's agent*

BERKLEY MEDALLION EDITION, JULY, 1965

*BERKLEY MEDALLION BOOKS are published by*
*Berkley Publishing Corporation*
*15 East 26th Street, New York, N. Y. 10010*

Printed in the United States of America

# CHAPTER 1

The big bay gelding stood quietly behind the screen of willows near the creekside, held motionless by the slight, steady pressure on the reins. The acrid smell of wood smoke drifted down the small stream on the gentle breeze, and the voices of men broke the stillness with an occasional laugh or an explosive oath.

Mixed with this was the bawling of a calf and the mournful bellow of a cow. And now Ben Stratton's nostrils caught the unmistakable stench of burning hair and skin. A brand was being burned into a tender hide, and whether it was being done legally or illegally was a toss-up.

At this stage of the game, Ben had no intention of butting in on anything he could keep out of. It was easy to get your tail in a crack by sticking your nose in where and *when* it didn't belong. He had seen it many times in many places. Let bad feelings arise between two factions, or between law and outlaw, and woe to the stranger who unintentionally got embroiled in the ruckus. Sometimes, it was enough that a man was simply a stranger and that he was handy. Men who hesitated to take out their feelings on a neighborhood enemy for fear of reprisals had no reluctance in nailing some outsider's hide to the bar, especially if that stranger wore scuffed boots, a battered old Stetson, and worn-out Levi's, and sat in a saddle of Civil War vintage.

See the wrong thing at the wrong time, or hear words not meant for your ear, Ben thought wryly, and somebody is liable to wreck your plans before you start by seeing how long you can dance on thin air. *That,* he could do without!

A slight pressure on the right rein started the bay in a turn away from the willows, then Ben froze the animal with both reins when the voice came from behind him.

"Set right there, feller, and see how tight you kin grab your hat!"

Ben philosophically reached up with his big brown

hands and gripped the brim of his hat. His mind was racing ahead and to all sides, but there was no way out of this except to see how the tide ran and run with it, hoping for a chance to get out alive, at least. He gently cussed himself for not having kept to the trail instead of following his damned fool nose when it smelled smoke down in the willows, and then he reconsidered the idea of whirling and trying for the man. That could be plain suicide, and suicide had no place at all in his plans.

Accordingly, Ben dutifully gripped the brim of his hat and waited. Developments were not long in coming. His captor raised his voice: "Hey, you fellers! I got a snooper over here! Come a-runnin'!"

There was a moment's silence, then a startled oath and the crashing of willows as two men thrashed their way toward Ben. In another moment he watched his saddle gun jerked from its scabbard and felt his sixgun leave its holster. "No need for you fellers to put on warpaint," he said in a mild tone. "I ain't aimin' to git in over my head."

"You're that way already," said the tall redhead who had snatched his Winchester. "Step down—real easy."

"Can I let go of my hat?"

"Don't be a damn fool," snapped the redhead. "Just git down, and *quick!*"

Ben let himself gingerly to the ground, being careful to keep both hands on the saddlehorn, then stepped to one side with his hands shoulder-high. "One of you better go over me for a hideout gun," he said. "I don't want nobody gettin' the wrong idee if I reach for the makin's."

At a nod from the redhead, a bandy-legged runt with a salt-and-pepper stubble of beard ran his grimy hands over Ben, then grunted, "He's clean." He glared malevolently at Ben, who towered over him by a head-and-a-half. "Good thing, too!"

Ben Stratton gazed mildly down at the little man from his six feet four inches of height. "Now don't go to gettin' violent, Goliath. I ain't had my breakfast yet, and I'm too damned weak to give a good account of myself."

"Button up your lip, Jigger," the redhead ordered the runt. "Who are you, mister, and where you headin'?"

Ben grinned, gesturing toward his outfit. "Don't take much imagination to figger out *what* I am, I reckon. As for who, the name's Mike Johnson—Michael Alastair Johnson the Third—the same because my Pa and Grandpa, both of who wears the same brand, is still livin'. As for the where of it, you just let me fork that hoss of mine again and if you climb a high hill you'll be able to see my dust trail stretchin' long and far. In other words, trouble gives me a damned itchy foot."

"In other words, you use a hell of a lot of them," said the redhead. "Saddle tramp, huh? From where?"

Ben shrugged. "You name it and I've prob'ly had my feet under some cowman's table there. Texas, both ends and the middle—Arizona, Wyomin', Colorado, Californy—"

"You been to Californy?" the runt broke in eagerly. "Ain't that where they pick up gold chunks in the street big as your fist?"

Ben chuckled. "Only gold I ever seen picked up out of the street was when a feller got a gold tooth knocked out in a fight. Now look—" turning to the redhead, who seemed to be the leader of the three, "I told you how I stand on things like this. I don't know who you are or what you do or who you do it to, and I don't give a damn. All I want to do is ride on. How about it?"

The redhead shook his head. "Mister Johnson, you could plumb ruin a nice operation for us, and we don't aim to see that happen. Maybe you'd keep your mouth shut, maybe you wouldn't, but we can't take the chance."

*So that's the way it works out. Ol' Mister Stranger, you just poked your nose in the wrong place at the wrong time. Sorry, but now we got to bury that nose and you with it.*

With the suddenness of a lightning strike Ben made his move. Jigger, the runt, was the nearest to him, and gave out a sharp cry as the big, iron-muscled arm snatched him from the ground and crushed the breath from him. Ben whirled to put the small body between himself and the one gun that already menaced him, his own right hand snatching the gun from Jigger's holster.

Jigger screamed with what breath he had left as he saw the other gun come up swiftly. "Pardee—*don't—!*" Then bullets were thudding into him and his head dropped loosely to rest on Ben's arm.

Ben threw two shots with the unfamiliar weapon. He knew he missed with the first, but the second knocked Pardee off his feet, his gun skidding ten feet away.

Just in time Ben spun with his limp shield, putting it between him and the redhead. The redhead got off two shots before folding quietly down to the sandy soil. Ben stood watching for a moment before dropping his limp burden. He felt an unnatural warmth on the fingers of his left hand and raised it to look at the blood running out from under his shirt sleeve.

He unbuttoned the sleeve and folded it back to look at the raw furrow on the under side of his forearm. He went to his horse and opened one saddlebag, taking out the cleanest cloth he could find, which happened to be his extra shirt. With a pang of regret he ripped a sleeve from it, binding it tightly around the wound and tying it with his other hand and his teeth.

He retrieved his Winchester and six-gun and put them in their proper places. With a last look around at the still forms he mounted up. He rode over to the place where the men had their fire built. He got down to release the freshly branded calf, ordering it to "git" and watching with a grin while it dashed off to its anxious mother.

Ben kicked dirt over the fire and hurled the running iron far into the willows before again mounting up. With a last look back he rode on up the creek trail toward Longhorn, the town that had once had the reputation of a man for breakfast and two for supper. To say nothing of a stranger for an appetizer just about any time of the day or night. . . .

Ben went first to the sheriff's office. He found him to be a horse-faced individual with a luxuriant handlebar mustache and a bald head, sporting a violent red-and-black checked shirt that looked ideal for a checkers game. A hand-lettered wooden sign on the desk proclaimed in gold that here was Sheriff Asa Goodwin, and alongside the sign were Goodwin's boots, his long legs extending upward from them to the skinny rump luxuriating in the swivel chair. He looked up from his newspaper when Ben walked in, then looked a bit harder when he discovered how high he had to raise his sights to take in the whole man.

"Yep?" he said questioningly.

Ben nodded. "Yep."

Goodwin slammed down his newspaper. "Biggest damn poll-parrot I ever seen!" He peered a little closer. "Been winged, too, I see. Stranger, ain't you?"

Ben sighed. "Yep."

"Been fightin'?"

"Yep."

"Law ag'in it."

"Yep."

Goodwin picked up the newspaper in order to slam it down again. "Dammit, don't you know anything but yep? You ain't said another blessed word but that confounded yep since you walked in!"

"You said it first," Ben reminded him.

Goodwin passed a trembling hand over his horse face, letting the fingers trail caressingly over the luxuriant mustache as though gathering strength from them. "Set down," he told Ben. "Now, then. *Who* you been fightin', *when,* and *where?"*

Ben told him. Goodwin stroked his mustache thoughtfully. "Jigger, you say the runt's name was. And Pardee was another one. And a redhead. Sounds like part of the Black Butte gang. Been rustlin' cows around these parts for three, four years without gettin' caught—till now."

"You said *part* of the gang," Ben said. "Now I reckon I'll have to keep close watch on my back trail to keep the rest of them from gettin' even."

Goodwin nodded. "Could be. Wouldn't do for them to let anybody git away with killin' three of their men without payin' a price. Sort of dee-preciate their stock, if you know what I mean."

Ben grunted. "I know what you mean, all right. And I also know you must be a hell of a sheriff, to let a gang of cutthroats like that go along for three, four years in your bailiwick without wipin' them out."

Goodwin bristled. "Ain't *anybody* been able to root that bunch out of the Black Butte country. Cattlemen's Association detective took ten men in there lookin' for them and must've found 'em. Leastways, none of them ever came back and ain't been seen since."

"They been looked for?" Ben asked pointedly.

Goodwin glared at him. "You're danged right they've been looked for! Went in there myself and got lost for two days. Another day and I'd of been down to eatin' lizards. Never seen hide or hair of *anybody."*

"That must be quite some country," Ben said.

The sheriff nodded emphatically, parted his handlebar with both hands and spat accurately into a distant cuspidor. "You're danged right she is! When the good Lord got through makin' west Texas he took all the junk he had left over and dumped it in a hellacious pile, with Black Butte stickin' up smack in the middle of it. Little rocks settin' on top of big rocks, sand and lizards and rattlers in between. Say, young feller, you better go over across the street and let Doc Myers sling some salve on that crease. We can chin later. I'll send a couple men out to look them corpses over. Don't figger on leavin' town, though. There'll be some questions I'll have to ask you."

Ben nodded and arose. "Yep."

Goodwin glowered. "Git the hell out of here." Then his mustache twitched and he stroked it into submission. "Ben Stratton, huh? Name's familiar, seems like. Reckon I'll take a look through my wanted posters whilst you're gone."

"You do that," Ben said, and went out.

## CHAPTER 2

When Ben returned to the sheriff's office a half hour later, he found Goodwin scowling over a pile of wanted posters. "Found my handsome face in there yet?" he asked.

"I'm still lookin'. How's the arm feelin?"

"Like a fresh-branded calf's rump, I reckon. Sheriff, if you was alludin' to that scrape I got in down San Antone way, I got me a clean bill on that. Old Anse Marshall admitted he set his boys on me, so it was called self-defense. Hell, who'd think a little tap on the chin would break a feller's neck that way?"

"Hadn't heard about that," Goodwin grunted.

"You hadn't? Then maybe you thought they was lookin' for me because I took that saloon apart in Denver. Sheriff, I ask you—what would *you* do if the barkeep charged you for good whisky and tried to feed you panther spit, and then when you complained, he hit you on the head with a bungstarter; and when you took the bungstarter away from him and started lumpin' *him* up with it, some policeman tried to earn his free whisky by arrestin' you? Wouldn't you feel you'd ought to protect your principles by battin' the policeman over the hat with a bottle and gettin' the hell out of there?"

Goodwin slammed down a wad of posters in the same way that he had slammed down his newspaper earlier. "Why the hell don't you go back to 'yep'?" he growled. "Looky—if you're in this mess of papers I'll find you, and when I find out why you're in there I'll make up my mind what to do. Anyways, they don't send out a wanted poster for every barfly that has a saloon argument, so just set quiet and let me look these over."

Ben rolled a brown-paper cigarette and settled back to practice making smoke rings. Goodwin rattled through the papers, muttering under his breath and stopping occasionally to test his accuracy at the spittoon. "Gotta be here somewheres," he mumbled. "Never forgit a description, 'specially when it's about a feller big as a house, with blue eyes that're too damned innercent, pale-colored hair that sticks up like a hayshock, and has to ride a hoss big as a hippypotamus to keep from breakin' him down. "Hey!"

He suddenly stabbed a finger at Ben, stuttering excitedly as he dragged at a desk drawer, still pointing the finger at his target. He jerked out a sheaf of letters and began flinging them about, finally using both hands. He found what he wanted, naturally at the bottom of the pile, and peered closely at the written lines.

He straightened up and again stabbed the long forefinger. "You're Ben Stratton!" he said accusingly.

Ben pursed his lips, thought a moment, then said, "Yep."

"Then why the hell didn't you tell me?"

"Why didn't you ask me?"

"Ain't polite to ask a stranger his name! Anyways, I was so damned busy listenin' to you say 'yep' that I couldn't think of anything else. This letter's from Marshal Hooker in Abilene."

Ben nodded. "Judged it was. He told me he'd wrote."

Goodwin tugged so hard at his mustache that he made himself wince. "Shades of the devil and all his imps! You must git a lot of pleasure out of watchin' a man beat his brains out when you could set him straight with a few words! Oh, well!" He threw his skinny hands in the air.

Ben grinned. "Don't let it throw you." He looked around. "Anybody else in the place?"

The sheriff shook his head. "Turned out my last drunk an hour ago. Tarnation! So you're Ben Stratton!"

Ben nodded again. "Hooker told me you're the one man in this territory he'd trust all the way, so I headed for you straight off. Didn't figger on gettin' interrupted by a bunch of long-loopers."

"From what you say the interruption didn't last long,"

Goodwin said dryly. "Hooker says he was sendin' you out on somethin' special, but didn't say what."

Ben began building another cigarette. "Don't reckon you have too many special things around, do you?"

Goodwin looked at him hard. "You mean Hooker sent you out here to tangle with the Black Butte gang? Man, he must want to git rid of you real bad."

Ben shook his head. "I asked for it."

Goodwin stared. "You *what?*"

I asked for this assignment. You remember that Cattlemen's Association detective that didn't come back?"

Goodwin knit his brows in deep thought, then snapped his fingers. "Chambers—Frank Chambers. Small man, sort of. Real pleasant. You know him?"

"He was my friend," Ben said simply.

Goodwin raised his brows. "Ain't gonna do him any good for *you* to git killed, too. I tell you, Stratton, the only way that gang's goin' to be rooted out of that rockpile is with a small army. To be danged truthful about it, I was just as happy I *didn't* find them. A dead sheriff has a hell of a time runnin' for office again."

*"Or* drawin' his salary. In one way, it was a good thing for me to have that run-in this mornin'."

"How's that?"

"Gives me an excuse for bein' in your office. Tell you what. You send out those men to look over the dead ones, and I'll saddle-tramp it around town till they get back. Then you come lookin' for me with blood in your eye, as though your men had found out things I hadn't told you about. Sling me in your pokey for questionin', and that'll give me a chance to find out things about some of the people around here that might or might not be tangled up with the gang."

Goodwin scratched his head and then shook it. "If you're thinkin' I can tell you who might be mixed up in it, you miss your guess. Only reason I figgered the ones you tangled with *might* be from the gang is that they've just about run all the small rustlers out of business. Want the whole shebang for themselves. Then again, I'd heard there was a tough redhead runnin' with them, and it sort of tied in."

Ben leaned forward and put his elbows on the desk. "Tell you what I'd like you to do. Have your men bring them in and lay them out right here in town for everybody to see. Then you and some others you can trust keep a sharp eye out and see who leaves town in a hurry right afterwards."

A gleam came in Goodwin's eyes. "Someone hurryin' to tell his boss their bunch has been subtracted by three, maybe?"

"Just that. If possible, have him trailed to see where he goes into the rockpile, but *no farther*. Meanwhile, I'll be in the pokey awaitin' your displeasure, with you rantin' to all and sundry that you figger on hangin' me higher'n the moon for waylayin' three innocent travelers. Try to keep it secret that they was all shot from the front, however. Waylayers don't aim from that direction, usually."

Goodwin puffed out his skinny chest. "Boy, you kin leave the play actin' to me! Always had a hankerin' to tread the boards, but never got around to it except for gettin' up on a bar and promisin' all kinds of damned outlandish things if I was elected. Maybe I'd ought to want to boil you in oil, too."

"Want anything you want, long as you don't get around to it. I'm goin' over to the saloon now and sort of set the stage for you to come and get me. Takin' it for granted you got more than one saloon, which one has the roughest rannyhans hangin' around?"

"The Silver Dollar," Goodwin said promptly. "In that deadfall you can get a drink, a dance, a gal, and a fight, not necessarily in that order. Ain't a day goes by that someone don't git his hair parted by a bottle or a pool cue."

Ben chuckled. "Sounds like a real homey place."

"Depends on what kind of a home you come from. Me, I do my light drinkin' in the Drover. More genteel. They don't use nothin' but their fists there, generally, although once in a while a feller has to dodge a little lead when some hothead decides he don't want to bruise his knuckles."

"Silver Dollar for me," Ben said. "Don't forget, now. When your men get back with the bodies, before you lay them out, you come lookin' for me with blood in your eye. I'll put up a bluff, but you'll face me down with your steely eye and bossy voice."

Goodwin chortled. "Boy, will *that* open a few eyes around here. Some of these damned fools think just because a man's a mite careful about gettin' his carcass ventilated he's got a teeny little yeller streak, which of course *you* know ain't the case. Brother Stratton, prepare yourself to git stared down, and you might practice tremblin' a little."

"Don't need practice at that," Ben grunted. "All I got to do is remember some of the fool deals I've let myself in for and I shake like a gun-shy dog."

"How's the arm feelin'?"

"Toothachy, but Doc says he's afraid I'll live."

Goodwin got up and stuck out a hand. "Reckon I better tell you now I'm almighty glad to meet you. Might not git a chance to later on."

Ben shook his hand. "I'll be goin' by the name of Mike Johnson. Anybody asks why I was here this time, I was askin' about work on the ranches. Told you I shot myself accidentally cleanin' my gun. For a better cover-up, have your men smear dirt on them fellers before they bring them in, like maybe they'd been buried awhile."

"Will do. And I'll have the boys wrap them in some blankets so nobody can make a close inspection. See you."

Ben grinned. "With blood in your eye, of course."

"Mister, I aim to make some kind of a record for fearlessness and devotion to duty that'll make the outlaws shake in their boots and make the decent folks *ree*lize what a prize package they got in me. Oh—one more thing. You want I should write to Hooker and tell him you got here?"

Ben shook his head. "He'll find out soon enough, one way or the other. Right now you better start practicin' on how you're goin' to accuse me of murderin' three men and buryin' them in the creek bottom, and how lucky it was one of your men just happened to find their horses and go to snoopin' around, and how he found the fresh graves."

Goodwin watched the big man go out the door and past the window, and shook his head in puzzlement. How any man could choose such a life was beyond him. It couldn't be the money—lawmen didn't get enough of that to warrant the risks they took. Love of excitement, maybe, with the risks taking the place of the bottle with other men, or maybe it was just plain devotion to duty.

Whatever it was, Ben Stratton was becoming a legend in law circles. No job was too big, no outlaw too tough. He took them as they came.

Goodwin sighed and went back to his desk. Too damned bad some men had *all* the guts and others so damned little. . . .

# CHAPTER 3

The bartender of the Silver Dollar lingered after setting the glass of whisky before Ben. His gimlet eyes took in both the man and the blood-crusted shirt sleeve.

"Stranger?"

Ben grunted.

The bartender was thick-skinned. "Didn't think I'd seen you around before. Just ride in?"

Ben grunted again, a little more sourly.

"Hurt your arm, huh? Ought to get it looked at."

*"You're* lookin' at it," Ben snapped.

"No need to get huffy," the bartender said in a hurt tone. "You know danged well I meant by a doc."

"He already fixed it," Ben said in a more agreeable manner. "Sorry if I was snappish, but the damn thing hurts." He drained the glass in a swallow.

The bartender quickly seized the bottle and poured another. "Have one on the house. Real good pain-killer. How'd you say you hurt it?"

"I didn't," Ben answered shortly. "A man don't brag about his fool clumsiness."

The bartender leaned both elbows on the bar and assumed an attitude of close attention. At the same time the sharp eyes were taking in every detail of the man in front of him.

He saw nothing to indicate that Ben was anything out of the ordinary, except for his physical makeup. He saw the broad shoulders and thick arms, the deeply tanned face and blue eyes, all acceptable by ordinary standards.

But it was the hands that caught and held his attention. While big, they had none of the look of brute, calloused strength one became used to seeing in the cow country. Instead, in the tapered sweep of muscle, tendon, and bone there was a look of untapped strength that held a fascination for the viewer. True, they had their share of rope scars and calluses, but there was none of the gnarling and joint stress so typical of working hands.

The bartender took another look at the face, and saw something he had missed. It was an expression of quiet confidence, as though the battered hat and nondescript clothes were merely misplaced. Immediately the bartender stopped his overt probing. Something told him he had gone far enough. He found some glasses that needed polishing.

Ben looked around the big barroom. Goodwin had not exaggerated its roughneck atmosphere. In the far corner there was a noisy poker game in progress, the click of chips and flutter of shuffled cards a mere background to the cussing of the losers and chortles of triumph from the winners.

Down the bar stood four cowboys obviously doing their earnest best to drink up their paychecks the first day out, each one having a bottle in front of him from which he continually refilled his glass before it ever got empty. Ben had seen the pattern repeated in a thousand saloons in a hundred towns.

This was the initial phase—the cutting of the accumulated dust and boredom of the past month—the gradual exhilaration of mind and spirit as each fiery jolt took hold in the gut. Now was the time for bellowed laughter, for good fellowship and back-slapping, for catcalling at the girls in the low-necked gowns, for regaining the feeling of being one's own man.

With the quart about half gone the second phase of the celebration would begin, when inhibitions were throttled and muscles felt twice their size, when a man's a combination of wildcat, Solomon, oracle, and rip-roaring stud-hoss. This would be the time for the timid store clerk and peaceable householder to drain his glass, nod hurriedly to the barkeep, and shove the swinging doors from the inside.

It was also time for the barkeep surreptitiously to remove anything breakable from the bar and keep the bungstarter handy, as well as the ever-present sawed-off shotgun. Occasionally things had a way of getting out of hand. Chairs were replaceable, as were tables and dancehall girls, but backbar mirrors and expensive glassware were precious objects to be protected with the bartender's life if necessary.

This would be the time when an argument could start between the friendly drinkers themselves. It might stem from some real or imagined slight suffered in silence during the workaday month, or from a totally new insult, real or fancied, found in the bottom of a glass. Fists could fly, chairs be swung, bottles brandished and broken over heads, and in some sobering, tragic instances the heartbroken sobbing of a range-hardened man would be heard at the realization that the shot that killed his friend had come from his gun.

Ben did not wait for phase number two. He crooked a finger at the bartender, who came to him after a backward glance at the roisterers. "Where's a good eatin' house?" Ben asked.

"Across the street, about three doors down," the bartender answered, jerking a thumb in the direction. "Ma Jenkins runs it, does her own cooking. I'll give you a tip, though. Don't make any sheep's eyes at the waitress. She's being corraled by Moss Finley. At least, he thinks so, and he bows his neck every time someone tries to be nice to her."

Ben's lips quirked a trifle. "What does he do, spend all his time there drinkin' coffee so he can keep an eye on her?"

A shake of the head. "He has the harness shop across the street, and his front window looks right across into the restaurant. Sees anybody spending what he considers a little too much time over his pie, old Moss hightails over there and gives him the dog-eye. Not many men around look for a second helping of *that*."

"Mean, huh?"

"Mean as a sackful of rattlers. Man about your height, I'd say, but about twenty pounds heavier on a guess. Course, I wouldn't expect a man of your size to let anyone run over him." The bartender's eyes held an eager gleam and he licked his lips.

Ben looked down at him, his eyes cold. "You're nothin' but a goddam buzzard, wantin' to see blood but too yeller to spill any yourself. This Moss Finley must have cuffed you around a little, too, or you wouldn't be achin' to see him stomped." He pulled another coin from his pocket and spun it on the bar. "I'm particular what kind of a house I drink in," he said, and walked out. . . .

When he looked at the waitress, Ben could see how a man might get his brains addled enough to declare war on men he considered trespassers. She was of medium height but willowy, with brown hair worn in braids on top of her head and a pair of brown eyes that seemed to melt when she looked at any man, be he cattle baron or patch-pants dirt farmer. A small, turned-up nose made an attractive decoration above a generous, laughing mouth, and her husky voice sent shivers down a man's back even when she said, "Confidentially, the hash is lousy."

Ben looked at the menu on the wall, finally selecting the roast beef with mashed potatoes and peas. The big brown eyes went wider as the waitress looked up at him, who was taller than she even when sitting on a stool. "Double order?" she murmured.

Ben grinned. "I might be bigger than most, but my stomach's not. Might stretch it a little with that apple pie, though, if the first piece is as good as it looks."

"It is," she assured him. "Ma Jenkins makes them herself. She tried to show me how, but I'm all thumbs."

Ben had not wasted all his time reading the menu. "No you ain't," he contradicted her. "You sure *ain't.*"

She tinkled a laugh for him. "That's the sweetest thing I've heard this morning! Are you new around here?"

"Like a new-dropped calf. And before you ask me what happened to my arm, I'll tell you I shot myself while I was cleanin' my gun."

The brown eyes widened, but a quirk appeared at the corner of her mouth. "And I'll tell you that you don't look like a man who'd do a fool trick like that. You can tell the rest of the people that if you want to, but you'll have to think up a different story for me."

Ben shrugged. "One story's good as another, I reckon, long as nobody can prove somethin' different. Anyway, it didn't hurt my appetite any, since my breakfast was a hunk of jerky and branch water."

"Then you'd *better* have a double order. Tell you what—if you're down on your luck a little I'll stake you to the extra."

Ben grinned and shook his head. "I ain't that flat. Just bring me a regular and I'll see how I feel after I get that down. Thanks, anyway."

She smiled at him again and went to fill his order. A moment later Ben sensed someone sitting down on the next stool, and turned his head to see a dark, scowling face on a level with his own. *Ol' Moss is sure on the job fast,* Ben thought. *Ain't three minutes since I sat down. Wonder how the hell she keeps her job, with him buffaloin' all the males that come in.*

The black, angry eyes looked him up and down. Moss Finley appeared to be about thirty, with an unruly shock of black hair that gave him an Indian look. His hands gripped the edge of the counter, and they looked to Ben like big blocks of oak wood, hard and seasoned.

Finley's voice was deep and gravelly. "I take it you ain't been in here before?"

Ben turned to look at him full face. "You take it any way you like, it, pardner, but till I give you better reason don't look at me that way. I might think you're mad."

The black eyes blinked once. "I might be, at that. You're buttin' in where you're not wanted."

Ben looked around in mock amazement. "Why, I had no idea they didn't want customers in here. My mistake, I reckon. I'd better get me a tin bill and go pick with the chickens."

"You know what I mean! A man don't have to make sweet talk in order to fill his gut."

Ben felt himself becoming more and more exasperated. He swung around until his eyes were boring directly into Finley's, and a man whose senses had not been dulled by jealousy would have heeded the ringing of an alarm bell and backed off. But Moss Finley was beyond the mental processes of ordinary men.

He was a bull elk protecting what he considered his harem, and now, for the first time in a long time, he was being given an argument. His size was no longer a factor that made men hurriedly pay their bills and leave the restaurant muttering to themselves. This man was as tall as he, and from all appearances was in much better shape. It was evident that Moss Finley had felt his reputation in need of a refurbishing and had taken this opportunity to give it a polishing. A victory over this man would do it.

Ben had figured this out within seconds after Moss sat down next to him. In a way he felt sorry for the man, who was obviously the victim of a malady as old as man himself, and wanted to avoid hostilities if possible. But he could tell from the hot stare that this was a forlorn hope. Moss Finley was on the prod, and nothing would satisfy him but the crunch of his big knuckles in someone's face—namely, Ben's.

Now that he had the complete picture, Ben grinned good-naturedly. "Tell you what. You seem to want my hide, and I reckon about all I can do is give you a chance to take as much of it off as you're able. However, a man can't put up a good show on an empty gut, and mine's empty as last year's bird's nest. How about you goin' back where you came from while I eat, and then I'll walk out in the middle of the street and wait for you? Fair enough?"

The restaurant was silent as a tomb while customers and those behind the counter waited for Moss's reply. In most other incidences, Moss had dispensed with all formality, his usual procedure being to snatch a man from his stool, if he was small enough to handle that way, and hurl him out through the door, open or not. If he was a larger man, one blow from a ham-like fist was usually sufficient to reduce the victim to a dragging-out state.

Ma Jenkins, especially, breathed a sigh of relief when Moss grudgingly nodded assent. Her mind's eye could see the shambles these two behemoths could make of her trim little restaurant if they started battering each other around the place. She hurriedly came forward to clinch the deal.

"You go on, now, Moss," she urged. "I swear, if you start anything in here and bust up my place, I'll take a scattergun to you. You've hurt my business enough as it is, and I'll have no more of it. You go on, now. The man said he'd meet you."

Moss arose and hitched up his pants over a belly that showed more bulge than muscle, and continued to glower at Ben. "You be there, mister, or I'll come lookin' for you."

Ben kept his good-natured grin. "You won't have to look far, friend. Just to the middle of the street." He watched the burly figure until it disappeared into the harness shop, then turned his attention to the plate of food the waitress set in front of him.

She had been silently taking it all in, standing tense and expectant beside the big wood stove in the cooking alcove. Now she stood looking at Ben, a strange gleam in her eyes. Her voice had a breathless quality as she asked, "Do you think you can beat him?"

Ben surveyed her unemotionally. "Do you think I can?"

"I don't know. Moss has done nothing but fight all his life, and he knows every dirty trick there is."

Ben shrugged as he speared a chunk of roast beef. "Maybe I can teach him a few new ones, if that's the way he likes it."

Her hand darted out and rested momentarily on his left wrist. There was an edge of venom in her voice. "Beat him, stranger!" The voice was low but urgent. "Beat him till he has to *crawl* back into that shop of his!"

Ben's headshake was one of puzzlement. "I thought he was your gentleman friend—at least, that's what I was told. Seems you're the second one I've found in the last few minutes that would like to see Finley eatin' dust."

"There are a lot more," she said bitterly. "When a man goes through life simply grabbing everything he wants . . ."

"Includin' women," Ben finished for her.

She flushed slightly. "Including women. I came here to work six months ago, and I haven't drawn an easy breath since. Neither have the men who even smile at me."

Ben chewed in silence for a moment, then washed down with a gulp of coffee. "I don't want people gettin' the wrong idea," he told her finally. "I ain't fightin' this man because of what he's done to people in the town. With me it's self-protection. If I don't go out there and tangle with him now I'll have to do it later, since that's what he's after. If I do somebody else a favor along with it, that's all right."

"What's your name?" she asked.

"Mike Johnson. Ask me where I'm from and I'll tell you everywhere. Don't matter, anyway."

Ben finished his meal and reached into his pocket. Ma Jenkins, a peppery little woman with iron-gray hair and nose-pincher glasses, waved him off. "If you lick Moss it's on the house, and if you don't you'll need it to buy hoss liniment. Prob'ly need some of that, win or lose with that big brute."

Ben touched the brim of his hat. He unbuckled his gun belt and handed it to her. "Likely won't be needin' this, so you keep it for me. Be back after it in a few minutes."

Ma smiled broadly. "Nothin' like confidence, I always say. I see Moss is at his front door already."

Ben looked across the street and saw Moss bulking huge and rocklike behind the glass-fronted door. *Well, let's get this over with. Tough way to worm your way into a town—lock horns with the toughest bull they got around.*

He hitched up his pants over a belly hard and flat as a washboard and stepped out onto the sidewalk.

## CHAPTER 4

When Ben reached the street he saw that the news had already spread through the length and breadth of the town. The boardwalks on both sides of the street were lined with men and women waiting for the show.

Ben looked neither to right nor left as he paced slowly out to the middle of the street and stopped, his fingers busy rolling his after-eating smoke. He lit it and took a deep puff just as the door of the harness shop opened and Moss Finley stood in the doorway. Finley stood there for several seconds, looked up and down the street and then back to Ben.

"You can still save yourself a lickin' if you want to get on your horse and ride out," he called to Ben.

Ben took a slow, deep drag on his cigarette before answering. "That's right nice of you, but I've got some business to take care of in this town. Besides, I don't like anyone runnin' a sandy on me. When I leave a place, it's because *I* want to go, not because somebody don't like my company."

Moss took off his hat, tossing it back into the doorway. "You touched on it right there," he said. "I don't like your company and I aim to get rid of it. How do you want it, fair stand-up or knuckle-and-skull?"

Ben flipped away his cigarette after another slow puff. "That last sounds all right to me. My knuckles and your skull. Any time you say, brother."

Moss had been edging slowly forward, and at Ben's last remark he went into action. Lowering his head, he extended both arms and lunged toward the lighter man, wanting to butt the wind out of him and at the same time come to grips, where his superior weight would tell.

With a burst of speed almost unbelievable for a man his size, Ben side-stepped and his left fist whipped in a short arc like the strike of a rattler. Moss stopped dead in his tracks as the iron-hard knuckles blasted his nose flat against his face. Blood spurted down over his face and shirt front, and in the first few seconds of the fight he looked like he had been watching a butcher too closely.

Ben stepped back to let Moss wipe the streaming tears from his eyes and reorient himself. "Don't blow that nose," he told Moss almost gently, "or you'll pop your eyes shut tight as a bull's nose in fly time." He jerked his head back barely in time to keep it from being torn off by a tremendous roundhouse swing.

"Lucky!" Moss grunted. "That's what you was—*lucky!* We'll see whose eyes get closed!" Again he turned loose a mightly blow, churning the air where Ben's head had been. A split second later he felt a stunning concussion just under his left eye as Ben pistoned a right hand at him.

" 'Smatter, Moss—you mad at the air or somethin'—beatin' up on it thataway?" someone catcalled. Moss gritted his teeth and again rushed Ben. When he almost reached him he stopped short and lashed out with a broad-toed shoe, catching Ben squarely on the kneecap.

Ben involuntarily jackknifed under the sudden pain, and in a split second he was caught in those bearlike arms. He felt as though he had been snatched up by a cider press.

Moss Finley let out an explosive grunt, then a chuckle as he put on the pressure, his arms around Ben's chest and his clenched hands digging into Ben's back. "Now we'll see how the cow et the cabbage!"

Ben wasted none of his fast-dwindling breath on chuckles or talk. Instead, he pressed his stiffened thumb into the angle of Finley's jaw where it joined the bull neck, reaching around with the other hand to help lever it into the soft tissues. He felt the paralyzing bear-hug begin to falter as the nerves and blood vessels were mashed and constricted by the digging thumb, and jabbed deeper.

Moss roared like a wounded buffalo and tried to jerk his neck out of reach. When he saw he could not do that, he suddenly released Ben and clubbed at him with a right hand, driving his knuckles into the muscle-ribbed belly.

Moss had made his big mistake. The blow merely sent Ben back a couple of feet, giving him punching room. Ben felt his injured knee start to buckle on him, and quickly shifted his weight to his right leg. Moss was still coming forward under his own momentum when the heel of Ben's hand rammed into his forehead, snapping his head back.

Ben then hit him with a short right chop in the place where the best-trained man cannot take a punch—in the Adam's apple. He felt the crunch of cartilage, then Moss was falling like a chopped-down tree, his hands pawing at his throat.

Ben caught him and lowered him to the dusty street as though he were a friend who had merely tripped and fallen. "Lay easy," he told Moss. "You'll get your breath back in a minute. Just don't fight for it."

Moss lay gasping for nearly a minute, his barrel chest heaving for the air he could not get. Then the tenseness eased and he gulped in great breaths of air, his smoldering eyes fixed on Ben's impassive face. "Lucky," he croaked. "Plain lucky is all. I'll get you next time."

Ben shrugged. "If you want a next time I'll be around.

Better wear an iron collar, though." Then he grinned. "Reckon I better get me a couple lengths of stovepipe to wear over my legs, too." He rubbed his kneecap, which was just beginning to ease off. "You kick like a Missouri mockin'bird."

Moss struggled to his feet, having to hold to a hitchrail to remain upright. Ben knew how he felt. He had been punched in the Adam's apple himself and remembered the general weakening effect of it.

People had left the boardwalks and crowded close, awe in their eyes as they witnessed the humiliation of the town bully. Moss glowered at them, and more than one fell back into the group. "Some of you might not be so smart later on," he growled, then turned to Ben. "You keep away from Glory, you hear? I hear about you hangin' around her I'll stomp out your liver!"

"Seems to me you just had a chance to do that," Ben said. "Somethin' else you might remember—where I come from we stomp each *other*. I've got to eat while I'm in this man's town, so if you want to make this a regular thing for breakfast, dinner, and supper I reckon I can stand it."

Moss turned and tramped into his shop, slamming the door behind him. Ben felt a heavy hand on his shoulder.

"So!" Sheriff Asa Goodwin snapped as he turned Ben around and stepped back. "First day in town and you go to makin' trouble! I had you spotted for a no-good the minute I laid eyes on you."

"I didn't start this, sheriff!" Ben protested. "Anyone can tell you that other feller did. All I did was protect myself!"

A babble of voices broke out, all supporting Ben's statement. "Ol' Moss got just what he's been askin' for for a long time," one man said. "Just so happens this stranger's the one that could give it to him."

Goodwin turned back to Ben, looking slightly mollified. "What's your name, feller?"

"Mike Johnson," Ben answered, almost meekly. "Just ridin' through lookin' for work and I thought I'd stick around town for a couple, three days to see if I could catch on."

"All right," Goodwin said. "You stick around and look for work if you want to, but if I ketch you gettin' in any more trouble I'll sling you in the jug so fast it'll make your hair curl. Understand?"

Ben turned away, muttering under his breath.

"What's that you said?" Goodwin demanded sharply.

"I said why don't you tell the other feller that? Seems to me a stranger ought to be showed a little manners instead of somebody jumpin' him before he even slaps the trail dust off'n his pants."

"You never mind about that, and remember what I said." Goodwin turned and stalked back toward his office, the perfect picture of a stern minion of the law.

"What you reckon's got into ol' Ace Goodwin?" a grizzled old broken-down bronc rider said, reaching up under his hat to scratch his head with a horny forefinger. "Acts like he's been eatin' raw meat and gunpowder. Took that big feller by the shoulder, he did, and turned him around so's he could talk to him. Bad business, takin' hold of a man from behind thataway. I sort of expected ol' Ace to imitate the birds. That feller could throw him plumb away."

"Mike Johnson," mused the man he was talking to. "New one on me. Ever see the like, the way he took Moss's punch in the gut and didn't even blink? Then give ol' Moss a drink of Adam's-apple cider. Didn't seem to hit him hard, either. Just sort of chopped him." The speaker experimentally popped himself across the Adam's apple with the forefinger side of his hand, then gasped and clutched his throat. "Whew, boy! That *hurts!* That calls for some of Hank Manning's soothin' sirup!" He turned and staggered off toward the Silver Dollar.

Ben retrieved his gunbelt from Ma Jenkins. She peered at him over her specs. "What did old lean and lanky want?"

"You mean the sheriff? He was just protectin' the helpless town citizens from the outside riff-raff. If I go to pickin' any more fights I'm to be slung in the *calabozo* for anywhere up to life."

Ma snorted. "I always did say that man's brains was addled, and this proves it. Pickin' fights, indeed! When somebody has to pick a fight with Moss Finley the cows will all sprout wings and then God help us all. How's about a cup of coffee and another hunk of pie?"

Ben shook his head. "Thanks, but I'm plumb full, ma'am. Maybe you could tell me about somebody lookin' for a rider, though. I need a job worse'n I care to admit."

Ma was sympathetic but realistic. "Things have been pretty slow around here lately, what with the heavy freeze last winter and cows disappearin' like sand down a rat-hole. People just don't hardly have the money or work to hire any extra riders."

"What do you mean, cows disappearin'?"

"Just that. A man might go out and count his cows today and find he's got a thousand. Day after tomorrow he might be lucky to tally half that many."

"What's the sheriff doin' about it?"

Ma Jenkins' lips tightened. "Just what he does about everything else that takes a little guts. Settin' in his office waitin' for the thieves to come in and give themselves up. That's what surprised everybody awhile ago—*him* comin' out there and bracin' you the way he did."

"Maybe he has reasons the rest of you don't know about for layin' low. Well, thank you, ma'am." Ben noted that the waitress had disappeared. Ma saw his searching glance around the place.

"She left for a little while just after you got through lickin' Moss," she told him. "She'll be back in a few minutes if you want to see her."

Ben grinned and shook his head. "Next time I might not be so lucky with Moss. That feller's strong enough to make a livin' movin' pianos single-handed."

"Most of his muscle's in his head," Ma said disgustedly. "Can't seem to get it straight in his mind that Glory's just bein' friendly with people, and they're friendly in turn. No harm in that, but to hear Moss holler a body'd think every man that comes in is out to besmirch her honor, as if she wasn't capable of decidin' such things for herself."

Ben left the restaurant and headed back for the Silver Dollar. He glanced at the front of Moss Finley's saddle shop, seeing that the door was closed and Moss not in sight behind the glass door.

At the bar, several men crowded up and offered to buy the drinks. "Just what this town's been needin'," one of them declared. "Moss has been runnin' roughshod over folks long enough, and I don't mean just on account of Glory. He's come to think the whole shootin' match belongs to him and he's doin' the rest of us a favor by lettin' us breathe his air."

"Well, he can have all his air back soon's I can get me a job," Ben said, raising his glass in salute to the buyer. "Well, here's to women, God bless 'em. There's more fightin' over them than cows and money put together."

"Amen!" A thin, sallow-faced man raised his glass alongside Ben's. "Anyway, you can say that around here.

We've got more money and cow trouble than woman trouble, but there's damn little being done about it."

"Your sheriff seems to be a man that would take care of things," Ben pointed out. "He sure let me know where I stood, and quick."

"Don't know what got into Ace," one man said, shaking his head in disbelief. "Ordinary, even if two drunks start a ruckus you can't find hide nor hair of him. He like to made the whole town drop dead when he come at you like a catamount."

"Maybe he likes 'em big," Ben said. "What's your cow and money trouble you spoke about?"

The thin man shrugged. "Just that. They go together." A man can't keep anything in the bank if he can't keep his cows on the range. And if he don't have anything in the bank, he can't replace the cows that are run off."

"Run off?"

The thin man set his glass down carefully. "Mister . . . Johnson, wasn't it? A few cows *might* stray off into the rough country and go wild. A few might die of screw-worm. A few *might* die off from a dozen different causes, and do, but they don't just plain disappear by the hundreds without a lot of help. Trouble is, nobody can prove anything, outside of following some tracks to the edge of the Black Butte country."

Ben took a sip of his drink. "Looks to me like you people have got some long-loopers clutterin' up the landscape. Don't you ever gang up and go lookin' for them?"

The thin man, who had introduced himself as Henry Adkins, looked as though his drink had suddenly taken on a bitter taste. "Just *try* to get these people to get together on *anything!* They want to depend on the sheriff, and you've already been told what he's like."

"What about the Association? Seems to me they could get some action on a thing like this."

Adkins told him of Frank Chambers, the Association detective, and his disappearance along with his men. "Just don't seem possible that many men could plumb disappear, even around Black Butte. Sure, it's rough country and so rocky you couldn't trace an elephant through it, but—" He stopped and shook his head.

"Then it's your idea there's a gang working—a big one."

Adkins stabbed a finger at Ben. "Mister, I'll bet that if the truth was known it would stagger you to know how many men *are* hid out in there, coming out only to rustle more cows and get supplies. *Someone's* out to make a big killing in beef, and the way things are going he's sure to make it."

"Ain't there someone around that knows that country well enough to lead a posse through it?"

A white-haired old-timer spoke up. "Ever since I was a boy, and you better believe that was a long time ago, it's been all a man's life was worth to go pokin' his nose into that place. It was always a natural hideout for men on the dodge, and they didn't want anyone snoopin' them out. So, folks just got in the habit of leavin' it strictly alone. Hell, there's forty miles in every direction from the Butte itself that's all stood on edge and sharpened with the devil's grindstone. Nobody in his right mind would *want* to go there unless he had somebody to hide from!"

Ben nodded slowly, his face a mask of casual interest, but inside he was seething with the desire to get moving on it—to find out who did away with Chambers and make him pay with his freedom if not with his life.

In a way, he told himself, it was better that Goodwin had the reputation of being overly cautious, because such men as those who presumably occupied the Black Butte country would be inclined to sell him short. All Ben had to do, and he grimaced inwardly as the thought came, was to get at the spark of real courage he suspected deep in Goodwin's mind, and to get him to use it when the chips were down.

One thing. There had to be someone at the top. A bunch of men simply did not form a rustling gang and go about it hit-and-miss, stealing cows right and left without any concrete plan for their handling and eventual sale. There had to be brains to run such an operation, and ten would get you a hundred that those brains were not cooking along with those of the ordinary gang members out in the sun-baked bad lands . . .

And, another ten would get you another hundred that those brains could not be too far away. Emergencies had a way of arising, especially in large illegal enterprises, and at such times there had to be fast decisions made. In a pinch, a major decision could not wait for instructions to come from afar, so the big man *had* to be somewhere close at hand. If not here in Longhorn, then at one of the half-dozen other small towns scattered for fifty miles up and down the fertile valley that was the lifeblood of the local cattle industry.

Needle in a haystack. Those brains could be in any head in the valley, or, unhappily, outside of it. Ben deeply regretted the necessity for such straight shooting that morning. Perhaps a survivor, faced with short shrift at the end of a long rope, would have tried to trade with talk, but that angle was out. None of those three would tell anybody anything—directly.

Ben was pinning at least a thread of hope that when the three were laid out it might spark enough alarm in someone that he—or she—might leave town immediately to inform someone else of their deaths. But if the brains were here in Longhorn the plan would fall flat on its face. The news would reach the big one as soon as it would reach any other townspeople.

"If I had my way about it," Adkins was saying, "all the ranchers would get together and put on war paint. But it's not only the ranchers that are suffering. Don't know if I told you or not, but I run the hardware store here, and my trade has gone downhill something awful in the last two years. If it keeps up I'll have to shut off credit, and if that happens I might as well close the doors. There's practically nothing *but* credit business in the cattle country, as you know."

Ben nodded. It was a longtime custom to run your bill at the hardware store, the grocery store, and everywhere else that had items vital to ranch operation, and then pay off in lump sums when the cattle went to market and were paid for. It was a vicious circle. The ranchers could not operate without credit, and the merchants could not give credit without at least the prospect of being paid. And a rancher without enough cows left to show a profit was up a stump for sure.

It could be a big cattleman, whose shipments of many head of cattle would arouse no suspicion. It might be a business man, skilled in the ways of merchandising and concealment of profits. And, it could well be someone who was neither of these—a retiring, seldom-seen person, or one whose public life was so mediocre that it would excite no suspicion.

Ben could see that the job laid out for him was not going to be an easy one. That it could prove extremely dangerous was evidenced by his encounter with the three men that morning, and the mysterious fate of Chambers and his men. He wondered how Adkins would stack up if it came to a showdown. Many men talked a hell of a good war but were gun-shy. Well, if worst came to worst he might be able to depend on the hardware man for extra guns, at least. That *might* be something.

## CHAPTER 5

One by one the other men drifted away to take care of one thing or another until Ben was left alone for awhile. The bartender came over and refilled Ben's glass from a private bottle he took from under the bar.

"Sorry I rubbed you the wrong way this morning," he said, "but maybe after meeting Moss Finley you can understand why a lot of us wanted to see him stomped, as you put it."

Ben nodded. "I can see, all right. Mean cuss. I was lucky enough to land a couple of good punches or he'd of stomped *me*. I take back what I said awhile ago."

The bartender leaned both elbows on the bar, a small smirk on his face. "That's not the way I heard it. They're saying you handled Moss like he was a wet-nosed kid, and I know he's not. He's a rough, tough son of a rough, tough father, and till today I can't seem to remember when anybody's even given him a good fight. Being a cowhand yourself, you know they're not exactly a bunch of ribbon clerks, and Moss has handled them as fast as they gobble Ma's pie and bat their eyes at Glory."

Ben nodded again. "Like I said, a mean cuss. That girl, now—she's quite a somethin'. I can see how a feller might lose his head like this Moss has over her. Thing is, though, she don't seem to be quite so took with *him*. Gave me that idea, anyway."

"Confidentially," the bartender said, lowering his voice even more, "I think she's been waiting to see him whipped, like all the rest of us. When she came here about six months ago she didn't know Moss from Adam's off ox, any more than she did the rest of us. She was nice to him like she is to everybody, and he took it to heart."

"Staked out a claim," Ben mused.

"You might say that. Anyway, she's told him time and again he has no claim on her, but it makes no difference to Moss. He goes right on with the sheep's eyes and the fists."

"Too bad. She might find someone she really likes if it wasn't for him."

"She did, but Moss beat him up so bad he was in bed for nearly a week. Young fellow named Marty Engle, works for Carl Morris on the Rafter H ranch near here. Marty swore he was going gunning for Moss when he got up, but Glory talked him out of it."

"Where's this Marty now?"

"Still working at the ranch. But he don't come to town very often to save trouble. Real nice kid, hard worker. Say, that's an idea! I heard just yesterday that one of Morris' old hands is sick. If you're looking for work, you might just take a ride out there. Probably won't last long, but long enough for a little stake."

"Nice to hear that one rancher has work, at least."

The barkeep grinned. "Morris don't worry much about rustlers. He's stocked his whole place with white-faces, all blooded stuff, and they'd have the devil's own time selling *them* if they stole them."

"Anybody else stockin' them?"

A shake of the head. "Carl's the only one that had the guts to try. The rest all said the white-faces couldn't stand the rough going in the upland grazing lands, but Carl don't seem to have much trouble. Anyway, he's ahead of the game. His die-off's a hell of a lot less than their theft loss."

"Sounds reasonable. Well, thanks. I'll take a ride out there this afternoon."

"Go west out of town and keep on the main road for about five miles. There's a sign where his road turns off."

Ben nodded and watched the bartender go back to his other customers. Over at a table in a corner the young cowboys were entering phase two of their celebration. Two of them were Indian wrestling on the table top, straining every muscle to crack each other's knuckles on the hard wood. The other two shouted encouragement to their respective favorites.

Ben left the bar and took a far table, carrying the bottle with him. He drank sparingly, sneaking most of each drink into a spittoon beside the table. The day wore on, everything lazily droning along except for the four noisy celebrants, who were rapidly approaching the third phase. Muscles having been tried and found not wanting, the whisky was fermenting into raucous, off-key singing, with the yelpers hanging onto each other as though trying to clutch the harmony a little closer together. Ben felt his ears assailed by the most outrageous racket he had heard since attending a Comanche wigwam-warming. His head began to feel bloated.

It was a welcome relief when the batwing doors flew open and Asa "Ace" Goodwin stood in the doorway brandishing a scattergun, his flowing mustache spiking out from his skinny cheeks like a steer's horns. "Everybody stay right where you are!" Goodwin bellowed. "Let's not have no trouble, now! I'm here after only one man! *You*!"

He minced toward Ben's table, the shotgun poked out in front of him like an elephant's trunk. "Put both of your hands on the table, stranger, and don't make a quick move or I'll blow you out from under that disgustin' hat!" Goodwin was playing his part to perfection, and Ben played along by slapping his hands hard on the table top.

"Take it easy there, sheriff!" he protested. "If I done anythin' wrong I'm willin' to listen, but if it's all the same to you I can hear better when my heart ain't up around my ears!"

"Never mind about that!" Goodwin roared. "Your heart's liable to be in some funnier places than that before I'm through with you, you danged bushwhackin' skunk!"

Men sat up straighter all over the saloon, and even the four roisterers forgot their private celebration at the despised word "bushwhacker."

"Now you just wait a minute!" Ben shouted. "That's a hell of a name to call a man without you got proof! Who am I supposed to have killed, and where and when?"

"This mornin' is *when*, five miles out along Dibble Crick is *where*, and how you managed to shoot three men in the back is beyond me, but by grab you did it!" Goodwin had worked himself up to a fine exhibition of thespianism, and Ben could have almost sworn he was actually being accused of the sneaky act.

Men all over the room were getting up, their feet carrying them slowly in Ben's direction. The damned old fool was carrying it too far! First thing he knew he could be dancing a fandango at the end of a rope, and the joke would be complete.

Goodwin, too, suddenly realized the turn things were taking. "Now you fellers stand back," he ordered, and Ben was fervently glad he kept his voice firm. "It's the law that wants this man, and, besides, it ain't proved yet he did it. Maybe I *was* a mite hasty, like he says. Stranger, you git over here to the door and shuck your gun. Lively, now!"

Ben moved, lively, while Goodwin's last words were still holding the men in indecision. Outside, he drew in a deep breath of relief. Mob violence was a most unpredictable thing and could break out over a mere suspicion. "Be careful of that damned greener," he growled over his shoulder.

Goodwin chuckled softly as they marched toward the jail. " 'Taint loaded," he said, and Ben nearly fainted. He had been on the verge of being hung—strung up to the rafters of the saloon—with the only thing between him and such a horrible fate a play-acting comic sheriff with an unloaded shotgun!

Ben was devoutly thankful when the door of the jail slammed behind them. "Brother!" he fumed. "You come within an ace of gettin' me lynched! That *bushwhacker* business did it. You could have just as easy ordered me to come along for questionin' and still show them how brave you were!"

Goodwin was still shaky. "Reckon I sort of let myself git carried away, at that. I'd never have forgave myself if them fellers'd strung you up."

Ben wanted to giggle, roar, and cuss all at the same time but took it out in one mighty snort, glaring at Goodwin.

The sheriff hurriedly put the shotgun back into the wall rack. "Maybe I better git you locked up all safe and sound before them fellers decide they gave up too easy. Got a good strong cell they'd have a hell of a time diggin' you out of, though. Anyway, I'll be settin' out here."

"With an unloaded greener!" Ben growled. "You put some hulls in that thing, by hell! If you don't, somebody might make you wish you had the bead filed off!"

"Dang!" Goodwin grunted, fumbling a couple of buckshot shells out of a drawer and shoving them into the shotgun. "Why didn't I listen to my ma and take up wood butcherin' for a livin'! Stratton—"

*"Johnson,"* Ben interrupted him. *"Mike Johnson,* remember?"

"Oh, yeah. Johnson, I just didn't think things'd take this turn. I had in mind the people would stand back and admire their sheriff for his guts in the face of danger, not decide to top off an afternoon of drinkin' by havin' a man for supper."

"Where's them deputies of yours?" Ben slumped in a chair.

Goodwin snapped his fingers. "By God, I plumb forgot! They're down at the mercantile store where they got them fellers laid out, tellin' all and sundry that they was dry-gulched! Say, maybe I better git down there and sort of tone them down a mite!"

Ben sat up straighter. "By God, you better! My neck's just as long now as I want it to be! You get down there and unwrap them stiffs, you hear? Let it be known to all and sundry, as you put it, that they all got their lead poison from *in front*!"

Goodwin rattled the keys like castanets in his nervousness. "Come on. I'll lock you in and take the keys with me so that—"

"Like hell you will!" Ben said grimly. "Somebody'd tweak your nose and you'd hand them over to him. You lock me in and give *me* the keys *and* my gun. I don't want to let it out yet who or what I am, and I won't till the last minute, but I'll be damned if I aim to be dragged out of a crummy jail and lynched by a bunch of righteous citizens. Or unrighteous ones, either."

Goodwin did as directed, then scurried toward the outer door. "Be back as soon as I kin!" he shouted over his shoulder. "Just keep cool!"

Ben cussed louder as the front door slammed and a key turned in the lock. He hoped that Goodwin would have the good sense to heave the key out into the weeds or somewhere, but that would be asking too much. Keep cool! With an aroused populace breathing down a man's neck, the icy shivers up and down his spine would take care of *that*.

Ben settled back against the damp wall of his cell, his gun in his lap and his eyes on the barred window and door. In less than a minute he was scratching industriously under his shirt, and shortly after that around his boot tops.

He cussed low and long. Eaten alive, by thunder! Then and there he made a solemn vow to punch Goodwin on the nose just once, even if he hung for *that*. A man could take just so much. . . .

## CHAPTER 6

In room Number 12, on the second floor of the Hotel Bliss, Longhorn's finest and only, a man and woman sat gazing at each other. Glory Lambert was still dressed in her waitress clothes, a pert little semi-uniform of blue piped with white. She sat straight upright in the rickety chair, unconsciously maintaining the posture that kept her body trim and willowy.

The man on the edge of the bed was a typical merchandise drummer, with a loud checked suit and slicked-down hair. By the foot of the bed reposed two large sample cases, each carrying the lettering, ALLISON'S IMPORTED GOODIES. Then, in smaller letters below; *Harlow Bassett, Rep.*

Bassett appeared to be around thirty, handsome in a garish way, with a prominent nose and eyes that seemed ready to melt at the first word of a pretty woman into pools of soft blackness or harden under stress to the glitter of coal.

He gestured with a well-manicured hand. "So what if this well-beefed stranger *did* put the kibosh on your persistent suitor, the right honorable Moss Finley? How do you think that might make him valuable to us?"

Gloria Lambert, her open, friendly waitress manner replaced with a cool, calculating expression, moved her own hands in a slight way that said nothing was sure. "There's something about him, that's all. He's *hiding* something. A man like that doesn't have to go around looking like a scarecrow, and there has to be a reason for it."

Bassett flicked ashes from his expensive cheroot to the worn carpet. "Maybe he's a real tiger in a fight but all thumbs when it comes to work. Maybe he can't get along with his bosses and can't hold a job. Maybe he lost his pile in a poker game and hasn't gotten back on his feet. Maybe—"

*"Maybe, maybe!"* she snapped impatiently. "Don't you think I have sense enough to weigh all those things? Remember, I've been getting along for quite awhile by being able to find out what makes a man tick." The smile

that now curved her full lips was one of slight derision. "Who brought *you* into the organization?"

Bassett's shrug admitted defeat. "All I ask is that you don't get *too* confident of your ability and grab a nettle. Just what *do* you think of this Mike Johnson?"

She paused a moment. "He's either just out of jail or he's running to keep out of one. And it's my hunch you might find more in those worn-out saddlebags of his than a spare shirt and dirty socks. Remember, I told you about his arm. *That* man didn't shoot himself accidentally, or any other way."

"It's been done before."

She shook her head stubbornly. "I'm going to follow this through and dig into him until I find out what *did* happen. Tell Toby to come in early for supper. I have a job I want him to do."

"Like looking through somebody's saddlebags, maybe?" Bassett hazarded a guess.

Her level brows raised a trifle. "What else?" Suddenly she raised a hand for silence. Outside in the hallway there was the shuffling of feet and voices growing more audible as their owners came closer. The footsteps halted near the door of the room across the hall.

"Can you *ee*magine that?" came a man's voice. "We was about to stretch that feller's neck for bushwhackin' before ol' Ace got sense enough to unwrop them corpuses and find out they'd all been bored from the front! Wonder how the hell them deputies of his'n got the idee they'd been dry-gulched? A blind man could see different."

There was a moment's silence, and the answering voice had a slight quaver to it. "All I kin say is, it's damn lucky for *us* that we didn't try to push the thing too hard when Ace told us to lay off. Why, that Johnson feller must be somethin' wicked with a pistol! That runty guy was shot *three times* square in the brisket, and the redhead and the other one just once each, dead center. Whoo, boy!"

The look Gloria gave Bassett was one of personal triumph, and he spread his hands in defeat.

There was, apparently, key trouble, complicated by too many afternoon drinks, judging from the thickness of the two voices. The first man continued as he jabbed at the door with the key: "Funny how that one depitty suddenly remembered he found the remainders of a fire and a place that looked like a calf had been throwed and mebbe branded. Danged if I don't think the main qual'fication to be a depitty sheriff is to have your brains kicked out by a mule! This damn key must of got twisted or somethin'. Can't seem to git it in that little bitty hole."

A few jabs later there was an explosive, "Hah! Gotcha, you damn slippery cuss! Come on in, Elmer, and be danged careful you don't knock that bottle ag'in anythin'."

Gloria turned slowly from her attentive attitude to face Bassett. "I told you I didn't trust Red and Pardee and Jigger. They must have been changing brands to build up a herd of their own and this Johnson stumbled on them. Knowing those three as we do, Johnson would have *had* to fight his way out." A slow smile grew. "And *how* he must have fought his way out! Five bullets in his gun, likely, and every one went where he wanted it, *and all he got was a crease! Harlow, we have to have this man!*

Bassett got up and tossed his cheroot out the open window. "Then get him," he snapped, "but be damned sure what you're getting. We don't want anyone that's so wild with a gun that he'll keep us in hot water all the time."

"He won't," she said confidently. "I *told* you he was a lot more than he appeared. When he handled Moss Finley like he was a rank amateur I knew he wasn't just some saddle tramp looking for a handout. Don't forget—have Toby come in early."

"Will do." Bassett came to stand close to Gloria. "May I make my apologies to you in the best way I know how?"

Her shoulder moved just enough to suggest a barrier. "If you mean by bestowing one of your educated kisses on me, the answer is no. The best apology you can make is to do your job and leave the thinking to people who are qualified."

He bowed with mock servility. "Your slightest wish, your highness. Do you want me to mention your Mike Johnson when I see Hugh?"

Her brows raised. "Hugh? Are you by any chance referring to *Mister* Andrews, your employer?"

An ugly look changed his regular features. "Don't get so damned high and mighty with me! I've been toting those sample cases around the country for two years and doing the best scouting job he could expect, and you expect him still to be *Mister* to me!"

"He expects it, too," she murmured. "If you don't think so, just try calling him *Hugh* the next time you see him.

And as far as those sample cases are concerned, I think it was extremely bright of him to have you supposedly representing a line of products that are impossible to sell out here in the wild west. That way, you appear to be quite simple-minded, which makes an ideal cover for your real job."

"Oh, I'm not arguing about his brains," Bassett snapped, jamming his hands deep into his pockets. "It's just that I resent being put 'in my place' every time I open my mouth."

"Only when you open it wide enough to put your foot in," she reminded him. "Just don't open it wide enough some time for Hugh to put *his* foot in."

He looked at her curiously. "So he's Hugh to *you*. What else is he to you?"

The look she gave him would have chilled a salamander. "When I feel that you have an explanation coming I'll give it to you without your asking. Right now I'll tell you it's none of your business, and if you're wise you'll keep it that way."

Bassett slammed a fist into his other palm. "What kind of a woman are you, anyway? When I first met you, you were sweet and loving as a woman could be, but you've gotten hard as nails!"

She smiled. "After you hook the fish it's foolish to feed him any more bait. The organization needed someone like you, so—" she spread her hands, "it was my job to get you. I got you. And remember one other thing. I haven't *gotten* hard as nails. I've been hard as nails all my life."

She went to the bedside table and took up the tray with used china and cutlery. "I have to get back or Ma Jenkins will wonder how long it takes for a drummer to eat his supper."

"You haven't told me yet if you want me to tell *Mister* Andrews about Johnson."

She turned at the door, the tray balanced on one upturned palm, a slow smile on her full lips. "No, I don't think so. I think that's a surprise I'll keep for him myself. It should be worth a nice little bonus to me."

Bassett mumbled something and turned away. She stood looking at his back for a long moment, then left the room. As the door closed softly behind her, Harlow Bassett threw his freshly lit cheroot to the carpet and ground it savagely under his foot.

"Damn bitch!" he raged in a hoarse whisper. "No more

bait for the fish after he's hooked, huh? Well, we'll see about that! She'll change her tune when there's a new boss. Wonder how she'll like calling me *Mister Bassett . . .*"

## CHAPTER 7

Ben Stratton was in a black mood. He sat behind the sheriff's desk stark naked. The blinds were drawn and the door locked, and Sheriff Ace Goodwin stood by looking wan and harried.

Ben's clothes were strewn over the desk top, all but his pants. Those, he held in his hands, peering closely at every seam. Every so often he would make a grab with thumb and fingernail, deposit a grayback on the desk top and hammer it to smithereens with the butt of his sixshooter.

"Easy on that desk top, Stratton," Goodwin pleaded. "I just had it refinished not two months ago."

"Johnson," Ben growled without looking up.

"All right, then, *Johnson!* But dang it, you've got it a-lookin' like it'd had the smallpox already! Lookit them big dents you're puttin' in it!"

"You're lucky I don't put some dents in your head," Ben told him morosely. "If you'd of got some formaldyhyde or carbolic acid or somethin' a long time ago and soused them cells with it the place wouldn't be crawlin' like it is."

Goodwin stroked his giant mustache for comfort. "Them things cost money, and I have a hell of a time gettin' enough to even *run* the jail, let alone buy luxuries like *that*. Why, if I was to—"

"If you was to heave a few of them fist-slingin' cowpokes in here and give 'em a stiff fine you'd have enough! Trouble is, you're prob'ly scared they'll sling *you* in there and let them damn bugs chomp *you* alive."

Goodwin bristled. "Ain't no cowpoke that's man enough to sling me in my own jail, I can tell you that! I'm an easy-goin' cuss, but when I git my dander up—"

"You'd likely go after them with a dry shotgun," Ben said, battering another louse to a loathsome smear while Goodwin winced. "The way things turned out, I not only didn't get a chance to talk private with you about who might be behind this rustlin', but I spent the most miserable damn night of my entire life scratchin' myself raw." The gun butt beat a rapid tattoo as it chased a fleeing louse across the desk top, and Goodwin clutched his head in both hands, moaning.

"Well," Goodwin said finally, "you know good and well it wouldn't of been smart for you to hit the street so soon after them folks was set on lynchin' you. There might of been a few that didn't hear about them fellers bein' shot from the front, or some that was so drunk they wouldn't of understood it nohow, and mebbe some that just wouldn't give a damn. Whichever, you're still alive, even if you *are* lousy."

"Barely," Ben growled. "Barely." Glancing down at his nude body, *"Damn* barely."

Goodwin could not restrain a chuckle. "Funny how a cowboy's face and neck'll be sunburned to a saddle color while his carcass looks like somethin' that's been livin' under a board, ain't it? Well, to answer your main question, I ain't got the slightest idea who might be headin' up that gang. Fact is, nobody's sure there *is* a gang. Some think it might be little bunches—like them three you run across, each bunch operatin' by themselves independent of the others."

"What about Frank Chambers and his men?" Ben pointed out. "No small gang could have wiped them out."

Goodwin shrugged. "Nobody knows for sure that they're dead, either. It's likely, but not *sure*."

"What else could have happened to them?"

Again Goodwin's skinny shoulders moved. "Could have all got caught in a landslide, flash flood, God knows what. Like I said, chances are against it, but it could happen. If I'd only been able to stay out a few more days—"

"Yeah," Ben said grumpily, pursuing another louse with thudding gun butt, "and if a frog had wings he wouldn't bump his rear end so hard."

He stood up and shook the pants violently, snapping the legs like a bull whip. "Reckon that's about all of the damned things. Seventy-five, by my tally. Sorry if any of your own little pets got mixed in with the bunch, but that's the way the wind blows."

"You can't insult me," Goodwin said loftily. "If you don't want gallopin' sand in your pants, stay out of jail."

"Why, you—" Ben started to wrap his pants around the skinny neck, then grinned and started putting them on.

"Aw, hell, I've been in worse jails than this, but offhand I can't remember where."

"Prob'ly in Texas," Goodwin guessed. "I hear tell they ain't got lice down there—they got tarantlers."

Ben yanked his boots on and stamped his feet into them. A few exploratory scratches later he was ready to go. "Might be a few strays up in the draws, but I'll get 'em when they come out to feed. Had breakfast?"

Goodwin nodded. "Long time ago. Gal in the restaurant was askin' about you. Seems she sort of blames herself for that ruckus between you and Moss, and she wants to see you."

Ben grinned. "She was just about to. Soon as I wrap myself around some ham and pancakes I'll feel like a man again instead of an old louse's home. See you."

He stopped outside the door and rolled a cigarette, his eyes busy as his fingers. Not many people were yet abroad, those who were mostly hurrying to work. Two men, however, were standing at ease against the hitchrail in front of the Mercantile Store, their saddled horses anchored beside them. They glanced casually at Ben as he passed, then resumed their talking.

Ben went first to the livery stable to see that his horse was all right. The big bay nickered an affectionate greeting as Ben rubbed his nose. The old hostler came into the stall.

"Hell of a lot of hoss you got there, mister," he said, then took a second look at Ben and added, "Need him, I reckon. Thought I'd ought to tell you I caught some feller goin' through them saddlebags of yourn. Hope you didn't have anythin' valuable in them."

"Thanks, old-timer. Anybody finds anythin' valuable in *my* saddlebags, I'll split with them." He took the bags down from the peg on the wall and opened them both in turn. A tight grin creased his mouth as he carefully inspected one compartment, then he refastened the flaps and hung the bags back on the peg.

No need to ask the old hostler for a description of the man. Ben had a sneaky hunch he would hear from him in person before long. Until then, he would sit tight and see what developed. Right now, though, the thought of food took first place, and he headed for Ma Jenkins' restaurant.

Glory Lambert flashed him a smile when he walked in. He nodded and sat down at the far end of the counter.

There were only a few people eating, most of the breakfast trade having been there and gone. She finished waiting on a man at a table, then came to stand in front of Ben.

"Mr. Mike Johnson," she said, leaning her elbows on the counter, the square-cut top of her dress falling away to show the deep cleft between her breasts. "You did what I asked, didn't you?"

Ben pondered. "I did?"

"I asked you to beat Moss till he'd have to crawl back into his shop, and you did just about that."

Ben dismissed it with a slight wave of his hand, his gaze rising slowly from the tantalizing view to her smiling face. "That what started Moss off at first?"

For a moment she looked puzzled, then flushed, and straightened up. "Moss took too many things for granted. To him, a friendly smile meant complete surrender."

"Your friendly smile could make most any feller holler 'Uncle' without any trouble," Ben said, easing the situation with a friendly smile of his own. "You reckon I'm goin' to be able to eat my ham and eggs in peace, or am I goin' to have Moss breathin' down my neck before I get my toast buttered?"

She chuckled then. "You won't have to worry about that part of it. *We* butter the toast. *And,* I haven't seen Moss since the fight."

"You will," Ben prophesied. "Soon as I move on he'll be tossin' his horns again. Maybe worse, because he'll have to prove all over again that he's the herd boss. If the fellers around town don't like the way Moss operates, why don't they gang up on him once or twice and cure him?"

"They tried it—once. Moss almost crippled all four of them before they managed to get him down, and after that he got them one at a time and beat them till they were a good lesson to anyone else that might have the same idea. Mike, all the people in town are talking about it. Yesterday was the *first time* anyone remembers seeing Moss whipped since he got old enough to fight."

"And that was prob'ly when he punched his ma for puttin' him in his high chair too rough," Ben said. "Well, there's not much more I can do about it. If I don't get a ridin' job in a day or two, I aim to move on. Old bankroll's gettin' mighty thin."

Ma Jenkins came with the huge platter of ham and eggs a few minutes later, and smiled at Ben. "Hear you come close to havin' your grub chute closed off yesterday."

"Ma!" Glory protested.

Ma smiled tolerantly at her. "You ain't been out here long enough to learn that we call a spade a spade. You notice Mr. Johnson didn't let my remark spoil his appetite none."

Ben grinned around a mouthful of tasty ham, chewed, and sloshed it down with some coffee. "If I let it spoil my appetite every time someone said 'Boo' to me I'd plumb starve to death."

"The sheriff said them men were ready to do more than say 'Boo,'" Ma said. "They're all sorry now, but that wouldn't have helped much if Ace Goodwin hadn't had the sense to unwrap them fellers and found they hadn't been dry-gulched."

At that moment four late risers came in, and the two women left to wait on them. Ben tackled his ham and eggs, mopping up egg yolk with his toast.

He heard the tiny bell on the door tinkle, and a moment later someone slid on the stool next to him. Ben stopped chewing and sighed. *Here we go again!* But it was not Moss Finley, back for more.

The man was obviously a working cowboy, with denims that showed work wear. He was pleasant enough looking, with a long, smooth jaw and gray eyes with laugh crinkles at their corners. "Mornin', Mr. Johnson," he greeted Ben. "Hope you are enjoyin' your stay in our fair city."

Ben pursed his lips and thought a moment. "Well, I can't quite tell yet, but it sort of grows on a man. About all I've seen of it so far is the livery stable, the jail, and a low-class saloon. Maybe I can tell you better after I've took a look at it from the other angle."

The cowboy laughed. "If a man can put up with what you have and still joke about it, I'm for him." He stuck out a hand. "I'm Toby Winters. Ridin' for Carl Morris."

Ben shook. "Seems I heard Morris was lookin' for a hand for awhile. I'm free and easy and don't eat much."

"Always a lot of grub at Carl's. And he *is* lookin' for a hand. One of our old regulars is down with the pip or somethin'. Want to ride out with me?"

Ben finished rolling the cigarette he had started, then arose. "Now?"

Toby shrugged. "Might as well. Came in for some stuff Carl ordered from the store, but it ain't come in yet, so there's nothin' to stay for. How about out front in ten minutes?"

Ben stretched and grinned. "Five. I don't have to check out of my hotel."

Ben went to the livery stable and paid his bill. The old hostler solemnly counted the money over and stuffed it in his hip pocket. "Never did git a chance to tell you about that feller I caught goin' through your saddlebags," he said. "Must of been he was mistook about them, him havin' a pair hangin' up there hisself. Anyways, Toby wouldn't hardly rummage a man's bags on purpose. Wouldn't need to, workin' stiddy and all that."

Ben gave a slight start at the name, and his eyes narrowed. He had considered Toby's friendly approach merely an expression of apology for the townspeople, but now . . . It was evident that he had been searched out—but *why?* Three answers presented themselves. Toby could be connected with some branch of the law, he was simply curious, *or* he belonged to some outfit that was interested in cultivating men who were known to operate outside the law.

Whichever it was, it was worth following up. Another thing came to mind. Marty Engle worked for Carl Morris, the bartender had said. It could be mere coincidence that the one man who had even partially defied Moss Finley worked with the man who had searched his saddlebags. At least, things were moving, and that was the main thing.

Toby was waiting in front of the restaurant, and they rode out of town together. "Be nice to have a bunk to snooze in for a change," Ben said. "I've been throwin' my soogans on the ground long enough."

"Where was your last job?" Toby asked.

Ben hesitated just long enough. "Panhandle."

"Pretty far from here."

"Far enough."

Toby laughed. "Good thing I'm not a lawman tryin' to get your family history. Forget it."

"Your sheriff gave it a good try."

"And got how far?"

Ben turned to look at Toby quizzically. "Well, he got a lot of yeps and nopes. Didn't seem to think that was enough."

"He let you go, though."

"Had to, when he found out I hadn't bushwhacked anybody. He always a fire-eater like that?"

Toby laughed and thumped the horn of his saddle.

"Him a fire-eater? Only way he'd eat it was if somebody stuffed it down his throat. Can't figger out what got into ol' Ace, unless it's because election's comin' up in a few months. Never seen him go *that* far to get votes, though."

"Maybe his breakfast wasn't settin' good. One thing about that jail of his—a man never gets lonesome."

"I know what you mean. I had one dose of that lockup and scratched for three weeks. So Ace didn't get far with his questions."

Ben did not answer, and Toby hastened to change the subject. "Ever worked white-faces much?"

"Enough to know it's like a rest cure after chousin' them Texas brush-busters. Morris a good man to work for?"

"The best. Good grub, good bunkhouse, and don't look down a man's neck long as he does his work. His boy, Charlie, helps him run the spread. Charlie's only about twenty, but smart."

"Charlie's foreman?"

Toby shook his head. "Not exactly. Sort of first assistant superintendent, you might say. Real foreman's Jack Quigley. Good cattleman, and knows white-faces like the back of his hand."

"Reckon they take a bit different handlin' than the cows I'm used to."

Toby laughed. "You'll get used to them, too. A sort of cow-nurse job instead of real punchin'. You ask me, it's a plumb pleasure settin' light and easy in the saddle instead of blisterin' your rump chousin' a bunch of wild-eyed Texas stuff through the brush and rocks."

"Amen, brother—*amen!*" Ben said fervently. "Lead me to that cow-nursin' job and I'll tuck in each and every one personal every night. Good grub, too, huh?"

"The best. And you don't eat stringy ol' longhorn, either. You chomp on white-face beef that's so tender your teeth don't even get a good workout."

Ben sighed. "Sounds like the Heaven my maw used to tell me about, only she had it populated with angels and cherubs floatin' around playin' harps and singin' songs. Don't know but what I'd rather have this one. How much farther?"

Toby nudged his horse to a slightly faster pace. "About one more bend in the road and you'll see the main house. Sets on top of a knob overlookin' the whole spread.

Reckon old man Morris, Carl's father, wanted it so he could look out and count his cows any time he wanted to. Must've had countin' down to a fine point, too. Wound up leavin' Carl the best spread in the valley—or in this end of the Territory, for that matter."

"Luck for Carl that old man knew cattle. How many white-faces would you say he's runnin' now?"

Toby thought a moment. "About twelve hundred, give or take a few. But that ain't all. He keeps them in the valley grass, but he runs a couple thousand ol' regulars up in the hills where they got to rustle for it. Sort of a backlog, he says, in case anythin' happens to his white-faces."

"You mean he runs plain Texas stuff, too?"

"Always has. Says he needs a few more years to prove the white-faces, and he wants an ace in the hole while he's bettin' his hand."

"Smart enough. Whoo-*ee!*"

The expression of wonder came from Ben when they topped a little rise and saw the Morris spread laid out before them. It was like Toby had said—a cattleman's dream, with a huge, rambling house perched on top of a knoll overlooking a vast expanse of lush pasture land that was dotted liberally with plump dots that could be nothing else than white-face cattle. Barns and outbuildings occupied their own leveled perches on the sides of the knoll, none of them of a height that would interfere with the view from the house.

Ben hooked a knee over his saddlehorn and just gazed. "Man!" he said almost reverently. "Think of the work that went into that house alone! Must've took a crew of men a couple years just to put it up!"

"Likely—likely," Toby agreed. "Mexican labor, I hear, with a Yankee boss. Well, let's go and report in. Gettin' somewhere around noon grub time, and that old cook makes the *best* biscuits."

Try as he would, Ben could not picture this man as being one who would go through another's saddlebags with any sinister purpose in mind. But then—one of the most cold-blooded killers he had ever come in contact with was a young curly-headed card dealer who wore a perpetual smile, even when burning down a man.

Time would tell, but in the meantime it wouldn't hurt to sample a dozen or so of the cook's biscuits. . . .

# CHAPTER 8

After the noon meal, Ben met Carl Morris. Morris was a tall, hawk-nosed man with piercing black eyes and a mouth like a steel trap. His handshake was firm and unhesitating, however, and he spared Ben a tight smile when they met.

"The job likely won't be steady," he told Ben, who had been introduced by Toby as Mike Johnson. "Old Hank Bedloe seems to be pullin' out of it and ought to be able to go back to work before long. You'll make a little grubstake, anyway."

"All I need," Ben said with a grin. "Gettin' so I'm afraid I'll fall through a hole in the seat of these britches and hang myself."

"Get some next time you're in town an charge them to me," Morris said promptly. "I'll take the cost out of what you'll have comin'."

Ben nodded. "Thanks. Might get me a shirt, too, if you think I'll be here long enough to earn it."

"You do that. Hey, Jack! New man here for you."

Quigley came over, and Ben could see why Morris had him as ramrod. Cattle savvy stuck out all over the man, and he had a quiet air of confidence about him that spelled authority. Quigley looked up at Ben from his shorter height, apparently liking what he saw. His handshake was brief but hearty.

"You and Toby roust around together the first couple of days," he said. "He'll show you the ropes, of which there ain't too many. Main thing is to remember you ain't chousin' longhorns and go runnin' the lard off them palefaces. Don't get off your horse, either, but for a different reason than with longhorns. *These* babies are apt to try and climb in your lap to get petted."

"He ain't foolin'," Toby said with a grin. "Had me a lunch the other day, wropped in a hunk of newspaper, and got off by the crick to eat it. First thing I knew, one of them critters snuck up behind me, reached out, and stole my whole damn lunch, paper and all, without me even knowin' it. *Then* she looked at me with one corner of the paper still hangin' out of her mouth and said 'Thank you' neat as you please. An old mossyhorn, now—*she* would have et *me and* the lunch."

"Never mind, Toby," Quigley consoled him. "One of these days you'll prob'ly get your lunch back when we eat *her*. Take Johnson out so he can pick him a string."

Toby led the way to the big corral that snuggled against the base of the knoll on the south side. It was protected from the north slope and from both sides by planted cottonwoods. "Carl's pa liked horses, too," Toby pointed out. "Put up a windbreak for them so a norther wouldn't sneak up and freeze them stiff. Don't know as we got too many animals that'll carry a man your size, but you'll likely be able to pick out a few."

Ben picked out a rangy claybank and a mean-eyed black that looked like he had a perpetual burr under his tail. "Don't know about that one," Toby said dubiously. "He's got a mean streak we ain't been able to work out of him."

"I'll work him down," Ben said complacently. "I'll just set heavy-rumped on him for awhile till he feels like cooperatin'. Don't reckon a man needs much in the way of hoss-flesh anyway to work them tame cows."

"Not much," Toby agreed. "About the only time you got to rope one of them is to get it the hell out of the way of a hay wagon or somethin'."

A tanned youngster of about Toby's lithe build came boiling up and dismounted with a flourish. Ben guessed this might be Charlie Morris, as was proved right when Toby introduced them. There was a certain arrogance about the younger Morris that instantly blunted the edge of Ben's usual good-natured liking for most men.

"Mike Johnson, huh?" Charlie said, more as a statement than a question. "Hear you cut a pretty wide swath in town yesterday."

"Wouldn't say that," Ben said, fishing out the makings.

"Hear you cleaned Moss Finley's plow. That's not easy to do, and don't think you got the job done just because you did it once. Moss has a bad habit of getting even, one way or another."

"So I've heard," Ben said, making a cigarette with deliberate slowness.

"You don't seem worried." Charlie was plainly exasperated by Ben's noncomittal attitude. "Ask one of the fellows that works here about the way Moss operates. Moss put him in bed for awhile."

"Well, goody for him," Ben said. "I'd guess he didn't outweigh this feller more'n fifty pounds or so, either."

Charlie opened his mouth to reply when Toby shook his head slightly. "If you'd been in town a little later you'd have heard some more about Mike, here," Toby said quietly. "The way I get it, three fellers jumped him outside of town yesterday mornin' and all got lead poisonin' for their trouble. That redhead we've been hearin' about was one of the three."

Charlie started visibly, then caught himself. "A gunslinger, huh?" he asked sullenly.

Ben did not even bother to reply, but turned to Toby. "Reckon it's about time we got to work, ain't it?"

"Yep," Toby said solemnly, then grinned.

"Pa tell you to work together?" Charlie asked sharply.

"That's the way it was," Toby answered.

Charlie jerked the cinch loose and slung his saddle over the corral fence like it was another horse. "Reckon I'll have a talk with Pa," he said, a trace of malice in his voice. "I've been needing another man up in the Rimrock since we put in the new herd we got from Bannister. Go ahead, Toby—show Johnson around, but don't go too far. He might have to leave most any time."

Toby's face darkened, but he rode off with Ben without a word. "That bastard," he muttered when they got out of earshot. "He needs a man up at Rimrock like I need an extra neck. For some reason or other he seemed to take a dislike to you right off the bat."

"He that way with every new man?"

Toby shook his head. "Just once in awhile he gets too big for his britches. Funny thing his pa can't see him the way he is. He'd save a hell of a lot of money if he could."

"How's that?"

Toby shrugged. "Mismanagement, mostly. Like sendin' twice too much grub out to line camps to feed two men, lettin' half of it spoil before it can be used. Like runnin' them white-faces in rough country where they've got no business bein' and killin' off a bunch of them. Like—" here he stopped and looked pointedly at Ben—"like sendin' an extra man he don't need up to Rimrock just because he takes a dislike to him."

It was Ben's turn to shrug. "That don't matter. One place is as good as another to earn your bacon and beans. One thing, though—the bartender at the Silver Dollar told me Carl had stocked his *whole place* with white-faces and that they seemed to be doin' all right in the high country. Now you tell me he runs regular stuff up there and keeps the white-faces down here on the home place. How come?"

Toby jerked a thumb over his shoulder. "That damn brat again. Persuaded Carl into runnin' them sissy cows up in that country where a *mossyhorn* has a tough time grubbin' out a livin', and like to wiped out the whole damn smear of them. Carl caught on just in time—this was two years ago—and set his foot down hard for once. They got off lucky, at that. Lost mebbe a hundred head in a blizzard, but they got the rest down here in time to save 'em."

"Ought to have taught Carl a lesson."

"Ought to, but didn't. Ever since Carl's wife died it seems he can't do enough for the boy. Sent him off to school somewhere in the East, but about the first thing Charlie done was get himself kicked out. Come home with a big cock-and-bull story about how the teachers had it in for him because he was from out West and was some kind of a savage, and Carl swallered *that,* too. Sent him down to Albuquerque to another school, and damned if he didn't last just two months *there!* Don't know what kind of an excuse he used on Carl that time, and I do know Carl was kind of short with him for awhile, but it blowed over."

"Pretty hard to admit there's a worm in the apple of your eye," Ben commented.

Toby nodded and chuckled. "Hadn't thought of it that-away, but damned if it ain't true. Reckon he *knows* Charlie's wormy, but just can't bring himself around to admittin' it. Well, heigh-ho. Yonder's a-wormy. Get out the salve, old-timer, and I'll dab a loop on the savage critter."

They didn't even bother to throw the cow in order to treat the open wound with screw-worm salve, merely holding her reasonably still while doctoring her. Ben grinned as he watched the old girl trot away. "Try that sometime with a longhorn," he said. "He'd of had both of us threaded like needles on his jabbers. Dang it, now I kinda hate to go up the hill and mess around with *them* again."

"Mebbe you won't have to," Toby said, an edge to his voice. "I got a little pull with Carl myself, and I might just put a bug in his ear."

Ben was doing a little fast thinking. Since finding out

that Morris also ran regular cattle, his obvious place to find out things would be where such cattle were being run, since they were the type being rustled. He might spend a month nursing the white-faces without ever running across anything that would help him, and a month was something he could not afford to waste. Better to go along with the tide.

"Wouldn't bother," he told Toby. "Might do me good to get up in the high country and have the stink blowed off me after spendin' a night in that *calabozo*. Anyways, it might be a damn *good* idea for me to be a mite out of reach, with that long, lean sheriff after my hide."

Toby was silent for a moment, then nodded. "Whatever you want." Out of the corner of his eye, Ben could see the long look Toby gave him. "Could be somebody else is after your hide, too?"

Ben turned to look at him calmly. "Didn't say that."

"I know you didn't. Only, most people don't worry too much about ol' Ace Goodwin bein' after their hide. He ain't what you might call a vicious star-man."

Ben faced him squarely and hardened his jaw. "If you're tryin' to find out somethin', just ask, and if I think it's any of your damn business I'll tell you. If you're on a pryin' expedition for that damn sheriff, you can tell him to ask his own questions and I'll give him some more yeps and nopes."

Toby waved a hand. "No offense. And if you think I might be scoutin' for the sheriff, think again. I wouldn't give him the time o' day, let alone tell him anythin' I might find out about *anybody*."

Ben let out a huge sigh. "Well, *that's* a relief! Should of knowed better, though. Man that'll go through a feller's saddlebags ain't usually the type to go runnin' to the sheriff."

Toby's eyes had narrowed to slits and his right hand was tensed on the saddle horn. "So you wasn't fooled at all."

Ben chuckled and saw Toby visibly relax. "Shucks, a man gets so he's got eyes in the back of his head and hears a hell of a lot of things that ain't there. Hears a lot that *are* there, too. Like an honest old livery man, for instance."

Toby grunted. "Thought I had him plumb pacified with my story about that. Well?"

Ben shrugged. "No well about it. You found what you

was lookin' for. Now what do you figger on doin' about it?"

"Doin'?"

Ben's voice was almost gentle. "Sure—*doin'*. You can't tell me you prowled my saddlebags hopin' to find a cache of gold nuggets, or mebbe some unset diamonds, and the *last* damn thing you'd be lookin' for would be money, knowin' how prosperous I *didn't* look. You *did* find that wanted dodger from California, though."

As he finished speaking, Ben's right hand made a blurred motion and Toby was looking into the business end of a .44. "Too bad," Ben said regretfully. "You're a nice feller and I've got to sort of like you, but I can't afford to take a chance on somebody collectin' a reward for my carcass. You see, I ain't quite through with it yet. Well, it's been nice knowin' you, Toby lad." Both horses had stopped, and the click of the gun hammer was thunderous in the stillness.

"Hey, wait, you damned fool!" Toby yelled desperately. "You shoot me and you'll miss out on the best thing that's come your way in your whole life! Hell, I wasn't lookin' through your bags for *myself*. I was *told* to, and whoever told me is the one for you to talk to!" Toby mopped his suddenly perspiring brow with his shirt sleeve. "Man, turn that damn tunnel some other way! I give you my word, there ain't *anybody* after any reward! If you're interested, *you're* the one that'll be gettin' a reward, and a *good* one."

Ben allowed the gun muzzle to lower a trifle. "Well, now, that sounds interestin'. Speak on, little man, and you better have your lesson learned real good."

Toby looked around, more than a trace of agitation in his manner. "This puts me in a hell of a bind," he said bitterly. "All I was supposed to do was keep you around so you could be talked to by *somebody else,* not by me. If I go ahead and tell you anythin', I'm stickin' my neck out."

"Your neck's away out right now," Ben said. "You was invitin' the ax the minute you stuck your hand in my bags."

Toby mopped his forehead again and nodded. "I know, but that don't help me any. If I tell you about the setup, I get my tail in a crack with the others."

"Others?"

Toby made an impatient gesture. "Yeah, others. This is no penny ante thing you're bein' offered, Mike. It's big—so damned big it scares me sometimes, but not enough to make me forget how big my cut is. And from what I hear, your cut would be a lot bigger."

Ben sighed and holstered his gun. "That's the way it always is—people pourin' riches in my lap and dressin' me in purple robes and stuff—in *words,* that is. Trouble is, I never *see* any of it. All I do is take a lot of risks and get shot at and slung in jail while the *others* rake in all the gravy. Some day, just once, I'd like to get my claws on some of the things I'm promised."

"You will this time, if you want it," Toby promised.

Ben shrugged. "Must be cows. Ain't anythin' else in this part of the country that's worth luggin' off, unless you steal some farmer's alfalfa patch."

Toby nodded. "It's cows, all right. I can tell you that much, but you'll have to find out the rest from somebody else. I've already told you a hell of a lot more than I ought to've, so I'd appreciate it if you wouldn't let on about that."

"Done. You wouldn't have spilled anythin' if you hadn't of been gazin' down my gun barrel, anyway, so that kind of talkin' don't count. Well, who do I see, when, and where?"

Toby's sigh of relief was huge and genuine. "That damn Charlie's complicated things somewhat, sendin' you up to Rimrock. Mebbe I better talk to Carl after all."

Ben thought a moment, then asked, "Any of our crowd up there?"

Toby shot him a look, then grinned. "*Our* crowd already, huh? Well, that's all right, I reckon. Don't forget, though, you ain't in yet. Won't be till you're passed by somebody else, but I don't think there'll be any trouble. Yep, we got one up there, but I can't tell you who it is—*yet.*"

"Didn't expect you to. Say, you wasn't lyin' about that ol' cook's biscuits. Reckon he'll have some more for supper?"

"Reckon. Well, let's give Carl his money's worth of work. . . ."

## CHAPTER 9

The last supper customer had eaten his meal and departed, and the final cleanup of the day was in progress. Ma

Jenkins and Gloria Lambert worked like beavers, scrubbing the counter and tables and kitchen work spaces, while an adenoidal youth lackadaisically prodded the floor with a damp mop.

"You git that floor clean or I'll skin you," Ma told him. "This mornin' I found chunks of grub and stuff where you'd pushed it under the counter. You want to go back to stringin' bob wire for a livin'?"

Jason Yocum shivered a bit as his skinny hands gripped the mop handle a little harder. "No, *ma'am!* I ain't lost nothin' out there in them hills, and I don't aim to go lookin' for it! I'll clean this dad-blamed floor till you kin see your face in it. I'll—"

"I don't want to see my face in it," Ma snapped. "All I want is not to see anything *on* it! Now you slap some soap on that mop and some elbow grease on the handle!" She wrung out her cleaning rag and attacked the meat-cutting board, muttering and grumbling to herself. "Eats like a horse and looks like one. Darned lazy kids . . ."

Glory finished her work and took off the soiled dish-towel she had used for an apron. "Guess that's it, Ma. I'll run along now and get ready. Mr. Bassett will be coming by for me in about an hour."

Ma shook her head. "I don't care what you say, Glory—I just don't trust that man. He's a city slicker if I ever seen one, and no good'll come of you ridin' that far with him at night. Why don't you wait till mornin' and take the stage?"

Glory laughed and patted her shoulder. "Mr. Bassett is a perfect gentleman. Why, haven't I been taking his meals to him in his room for over a week? If he was going to try anything—"

"If he was goin' to try anything he'd wait till he got you out where nobody'd hear if you hollered, like between here and Rockport. Every time I look at him . . ."

"Every time you look at him you see nothing but what you're looking for," Glory chided. "Now don't you worry. It's not very far to Rockport, and I can be with Martha for the night and all day tomorrow. Then I can ride back with Mr. Bassett tomorrow night and be ready to help you open up the next morning."

Ma grumbled some more, but finally gave in with reservations. "You be danged sure to have a good, sharp hatpin with you and don't be afraid to use it," she told

Glory sternly. "Ain't nothin' that'll discourage a smart aleck like a jab from a hatpin."

Glory went to the hotel, changed her clothes, and met Bassett in the lobby. He was the picture of the gallant gentleman until they were in the buggy heading out of town, then his resentment of their previous meeting took over.

"I suppose you have the bouquets all ready to throw at yourself for discovering this Mike Johnson," he said sourly.

Glory smiled into the gathering darkness. "Oh, no. I won't mention it yet, in case anything goes wrong. And don't you, either."

He snorted. "Don't worry—the last thing I'd be likely to do is promote any favors for you with *Mister* Hugh Andrews. All I want is my orders—from *him*. What you do is your own business."

"See that you remember that," she said sweetly, "and we'll get along just fine. How are the Allison's Imported Goodies going?"

Bassett's snort put the last one to shame. "Of all the damned fool things to set a man to selling—or *trying* to sell! Every time some rancher finds out what I'm supposed to be peddling he looks at me like I had two heads! Can't you just see these horny-handed sons of toil grappling with a pickled squid, or his equally horny-handed wife serving him stuffed quail in aspic?"

"You're *supposed* to be a ridiculous figure in this western atmosphere, and I must admit you fill the role perfectly. That suit—" She broke off to giggle maliciously.

"Laugh all you want to," he muttered. "A day will come when you'll wish you had something to laugh about."

She was silent for a moment, then said, "I wish I knew just what you meant by that. If I thought it was a threat—"

"I know." His voice was coarse with rancor. "If you thought it was a threat you'd set one of your pet killers on me—maybe your precious Mike Johnson, for instance, or—"

"Or Toby?" she suggested. "You flatter yourself, drummer. I wouldn't waste the talents of either Mike Johnson *or* Toby on *you*. You're more the speed of some chore boy who wants to start at the bottom in building a reputation."

Bassett clucked the horse to a slightly faster pace. "Like

I said, laugh while you can," he said. "*And,* don't send a chore boy to do a man's job."

Glory's glance at him was curious. "You sound as if you meant that. What have you been doing—eating raw meat between the meals I bring you?"

Bassett grinned crookedly. "Mixed with gunpowder. Isn't that what the old-timers say they feed a dog to make him mean?"

Glory shrugged. "Mean is as mean does. Now if you don't mind I'd like to look at the scenery in peace. I get pretty tired of looking at steaming pots and dirty dishes *and* dirty men in tall hats."

"How about tall men in dirty hats?" he murmured.

Glory's mouth quirked in spite of herself as she said, "*Touché.*"

On that note they lapsed into silence for the remainder of the ride. Deep darkness had set in before they pulled up in front of the hotel. The feeble glow of oil lamps from the inside illuminated the cobweb-outlined front windows, one of which boasted in peeling gilt lettering:

ROGERS HOTEL
*Rockport's Finest*

"Finest and only," Bassett grumbled. "Not a lock on any door and go after your own water if you want any."

"Go and register," Glory said shortly, "and let me know which room you'll have. When I send for you I don't want some snoopy desk clerk knowing about it."

Bassett had grown sullen. "If you want me for the rest of the night you'll find me in the nearest saloon. I've—"

"If I want you, you'll be in your room," Glory cut in, her voice sharp. "This is a business trip, not one for you to drown your petty grievances against me. And when I *do* send for you, *you come running!*"

Bassett's face was livid as he stormed through the door with his telescope bag and sample case. He came back out in a couple of minutes and snapped his room number at her, then gathered up the reins. "Now I suppose you want to go to your dear sister Martha's?"

Glory was stepping down. "I'll walk, I believe. I wouldn't want Martha to get a look at you in that suit. There might not be anything to the superstition of marking an unborn child, and then again there might."

"Thank God for some favors," Bassett said. "One of your family is enough for me. *Goodnight.*" He watched her disappear into the darkness and then headed for the livery stable.

Ten minutes later he entered his room and struck a match to light his way around. He set the newly purchased bottle of whisky on the creaky dresser, then lit the lamp with the dingy, cracked chimney.

For a long moment he stood surveying himself—a medium height man of medium weight, with a medium handsome face set off by a most ordinary crop of slicked-down black hair. All this mediocrity was heightened by *the suit*—that glaring, hateful monstrosity of black-and-tan checks that immediately made him the butt of jokes and whispered comments.

For that one long moment the hate blazed from his eyes, then died, and was replaced with a cunning that would have aroused Glory's curiosity even more than did his remark about the chore boy. *Let them laugh—all of them. We'll see who wears the checkered suit in the long run.*

With methodical slowness, Bassett threw his sample case on the bed and opened it. He rummaged far down in the bottom and came up with a holstered six-gun, its blued barrel ominous in the dim lamplight as he flipped it from the holster to check the cylinder.

He buckled on the belt under his coat, then shoved the gun back into it. He faced the dresser again, and assumed a stance of lazy nonchalance. Suddenly his right hand moved, whipping back the coattails and snaking the gun out in a draw of bewildering speed. The hammer snapped on an empty chamber a bare fraction of a second after his first move.

A small, lip-pursing smile came on his face, but he was not satisfied. Again and again he went through the motions, each draw practically a replica of the last, not noticeably faster but never slower. *If only they knew. If they had any idea that their checkered-suited comedian was in reality a wolf in cheap clothing, with fangs that were real and deadly!*

He crossed to the window and raised the tattered blind he had pulled before his secret gun practice. The muted noises of the night poured up at him: the high-pitched laughter of one of the dancing girls in the saloon across the street, the tramp of hoofs on the wood floor of the livery stable in the rear of the hotel, the vexed crying of a child somewhere in the frightening depths of the night.

Far down the street, Bassett could see the light in the second story of a house, and he ground his teeth. She was there, ostensibly to visit her pregnant sister, but in reality to contact Hugh Andrews, *the* man. While he, Bassett, was relegated to the ignominy of an indefinite wait in a ratty hotel room awaiting their pleasure. *Their* pleasure!

*To hell with it!*

Bassett again pulled the blind. He crossed to the dresser and took up the quart bottle, uncorking it with slow deliberation. With that same slow purpose he raised the bottle to his mouth and took three deep swallows, feeling the fire go deeper into his throat with every swallow until the final one made him gasp.

He held the bottle out in front of him and looked at it through the thin film of tears the fiery jolts had produced. *That* was the friend of man—an amber friend who just sat in the bottle and waited until needed, then went to work on a man's brain to make him any one of a number of things—all different.

Different from his usual self, that is. It would take away sorrow and replace it with joy; bring laughter where tears had flowed, make a lion out of a frightened man. It could break habits of a lifetime and make new ones, lift a man out of the muck into a hazy, pleasant heaven all his own—*but all for a price.*

Bassett reflected on that price as he raised the bottle again to his lips. The headache would be nothing, nor the queasy feeling in the stomach that would make the thought of food a revolting thing.

The dearest price was in being dropped back into the depths from which a man had soared—the realization that it had all been a dream, a booze-induced fantasy of aggrandizement that made the little man big only in his own mind.

*The hell with that, too!* At least there would be a short respite from his humiliation, a suspension of time when even the hated suit would assume insignificance, when a man named Bassett would be all he desired to be. And if *Mr.* Andrews sent for him while *Mr.* Basset was in existence it would be all right to. It could be no worse than seeing the man while sober. There would be no kowtowing from *Mr.* Bassett. . . .

Three town blocks away, Glory Lambert went to the door in answer to a knock. She opened it and smiled at the slender, white-haired man in the quietly tasteful suit who stood outside.

"Come in, Hugh," she said.

## CHAPTER 10

It was after dark when Ben Stratton, alias Mike Johnson, knocked on the door of the small creekside house where Sheriff Ace Goodwin held bachelor's hall. Over the tinkle of the stream in its rocky bed he heard the complaint of a creaky chair being vacated, then the progressive squawks of tired boards bending under heavy footsteps.

Goodwin opened the door a crack and peered out. The gleam of the oil lamp lit up Ben's face dimly, and Goodwin grunted. "Some folks might say it was nice to see you, but danged if I will. Trouble just seems to breed like rabbits around where you are."

Ben jerked the door open, slid in, and closed it behind him. "My, you sound like maybe somebody took your candy. What kind of trouble have I brought down on your poor long-sufferin' head now?"

Goodwin ran his long, skinny fingers through his thinning hair and pooched out his lips. "You and your danged idees about me puttin' on a show of bein' a rough, tough sheriff, that's what! Now every time some saloonkeeper has a ruckus startin' in his place the first thing he thinks of is sendin' for me."

Ben surveyed him critically. "Well, you seem to be all in one piece, and I don't see any scars or bruises."

Goodwin snorted. "Not *yet*! But that ain't sayin' what'll happen when the shock of seein' me gather you in like a ripe plum wears off. I've noticed quite a few fellers eyin' me like mebbe they didn't believe all they hear and wouldn't mind bracin' me so they could make a reputation."

Ben sprawled in a kitchen chair by the table and poured himself a drink in a cracked glass from the bottle Goodwin had been nursing. "Here's to courage and brains," he said, raising the glass. "If a man has one, he don't need the other."

Goodwin sat down, grabbed up the bottle, and jabbed its neck at another glass. "Man's in a hell of a fix when he ain't got either," he grumbled. "If I'd of had any brains I'd of locked the door when I seen you comin' that day."

Ben sipped his drink delicately, then made a face. "Where the hell did you get this panther spit? I've tasted better stuff out of the bottom of a Comanche water bag!" He held his nose with the other hand and drained the glass.

Goodwin looked on with an upside-down smile. "For a gink that don't like somethin' you sure make a hell of a good show of puttin' up with it. Hey now—let that bottle alone! A few more of them sips of yourn and I'll be fresh out of headache material!" Then he grinned. "It *is* right horrifyin' stuff, ain't it? Only reason I drink it is the price—which is free."

Ben grunted and belched. "Free ain't enough. He'd ought to give you a box of sody crackers with each bottle. Who is this enemy of the people?"

Goodwin gagged down a swallow and wiped his streaming eyes with a ragged red bandanna handkerchief. "Before God," he gasped, "a man has to be purty damned stingy to drink this stuff just because it's free. Why, right at this very minute it might be turnin' my blood into water and slowly eatin' my brain away."

"You said a minute ago you didn't have any," Ben pointed out.

"Well, it might be boilin' around in the cavity where it's s'posed to be and doin' no damn little harm. Still—" He eyed the angry brown liquid appraisingly. "Still, when I think of the price, a clean head cavity don't seem so damned important. Reckon I'll just go on savin' my money and plannin' on whether I want brass or wooden handles on my coffin."

"You could afford silver ones with all the money you're savin' on drinks," Ben said, calmly taking a big swallow while Goodwin watched and shuddered. "What's the news?"

"You asked me who the fiend is that supplies me with this popskull. I'll tell you that first so if I'm dead before mornin' you kin persecute him for my d*ee*-mise. It's old man Selkirk—got a cabin back in the hills a-ways. Runs a few cows and a still. In exchange for twistin' my neck to the east when I pass his place, and holdin' my nose when he's runnin' off a batch, he drops me off a bottle about twicet a week."

"What you need's a wife," Ben said.

Goodwin looked up in alarm. "What the hell for?"

"To pour that stuff down the backhouse and hit ol' Selkirk over the head with the bottle. Man, you keep drinkin' that and your toes'll curl up so damned tight you won't be able to get your socks off. Not only that, but I heard of a feller once that drank so much moonshine that it plumb pickled him. When he died he smelt so much like a still that no self-respectin' preacher would say the words over him, so they had to get the justice of the peace to come and declare him not guilty."

"Not guilty of *what*?"

Ben grinned. "Imitatin' a sponge. How-the-so-ever, I reckon if this stuff ain't killed you already you've got a little time left. Enough to tell me what's been goin' on."

"I done that already."

"I mean, have your men noticed any new people in town, or any old ones leavin'?"

Goodwin shook his head. "What the hell would that prove?"

Ben sighed. "Mebbe your head cavity's all burnt out, at that. If any new ones have come in, they might be lookin' for me. If any old ones have left, they might not *want* to see me. Ketch?"

"I reckon. Far's I know, the town's goin' along in the same ol' rut, nobody comin' and nobody goin'. Oh—there's one thing, though. Ol' Moss says he's goin' to stomp your liver the next time he ketches you in town."

Ben pondered a moment. "That has a familiar ring, seems to me. Oh, yeah. That's what he was goin' to do the first time. He say how he aimed to do it this time?"

"With them number twelve boots, I reckon," Goodwin said. "One thing about Moss—he's got a grip like a bulldog when he gits hold of an idee. *And*, he's got the idee you're out to take Glory away from him." He sighed hugely and shook his head. "An idee like that could lead to an everlastin' feud between you two, and the winner'd prob'ly be so stove up and ugly that Glory or no other woman would look at him."

Ben shrugged. "Well, I reckon Moss'll get his chance about tomorrow afternoon. I aim to come in to buy me some clothes. Mebbe I better see what Moss has on his mind before I buy the clothes."

Goodwin agreed. "Might tatter 'em up a mite, at that. How you like nursin' white-faces?"

Ben poured himself another drink from the rapidly diminishing supply. "Sheriff, if I'd of knowed years ago how sweet a job that was, I'd of saved myself a lot of saddle boils and busted bones. To say nothin' of the cuss words I invented from time to time, which prob'ly will keep me out of heaven permanent."

Goodwin rescued the bottle and helped himself. Ben arose and sauntered around the kitchen. "Nice little shack you got here. Any fish in the crick?"

"Some danged suckers and a few sunfish is all, but up where she comes out of the hills there's trout. I go fishin' every once in awhile."

"When some bad man comes to town?" Ben guessed.

Goodwin shot him a look. "How the hell'd you know?"

Ben laughed and set his drink down on the corner of the kitchen cabinet. Then, moving like a big cat, he took two long strides, jerked open the door, and dove outside, his body bent low, arms outstretched.

Goodwin heard a startled curse, then footsteps beating a rapid tattoo on the hard-baked ground. Before he could snatch his gun out of the holster where it hung on the back of a chair and get to the door, there came a high-pitched yell and a crashing in the willows that sounded like a bull moose on the loose.

Then came Ben's voice: "Hold still, you damned eel! You want to come along, or do I go back to the house with just your arm?"

Goodwin turned to snatch up the lamp before going outside. The light showed Ben forging up the creek bank towing a white-haired man by one wrist. Both were dripping wet from floundering around in the creek, and Ben was letting out some juicy cuss words about things in general and eavesdroppers in particular.

Goodwin peered at the prisoner in the dim light. "Danged if it ain't Harry Selkirk! What you doin' here, Harry?"

The old man swiped a shirtsleeve across his dripping brows. "I warn't doin' nothin', sheriff! I swear I warn't! I'd only jist come up to the door when this big buffler come boilin' out and made a grab fer me! Who the hell *wouldn't* run, I ask you?"

"You're a damn liar," Ben said. "I heard you prowlin' around for two or three minutes before I busted out. Now you talk up, and pronto."

The old man shot a hopeful look at Goodwin, whose grim visage discouraged any hope of intercession, then at

Ben before he shrugged his thin shoulders. "Dang it, sheriff," he whined, "you know I'm a poor man and I got to make a penny any way I kin—"

"You're poor like the man that sets behind the desk in the bank," Goodwin said brusquely, "but I grant you one thing you said is true. You'll make a penny or a dollar any way you kin. Harry, I've always treated you square, and if you want to keep a whole hide and keep runnin' free, you just pipe up and say what the hell you was doin' here. Right now!"

Selkirk sighed. "I might of knowed it was too good to be true. Feller tells me all I got to do is watch your place, and if I see a great big feller like this one come to see you, to listen outside and hear what you say. Then I'd let him know and he was to give me ten dollars."

"What feller?" Goodwin asked.

Selkirk spread his hands. "I don't know what his name is. He come to see me after dark and stayed in the shadders, so I don't even know what he looks like, either."

"Then how was you s'posed to tell him anythin', if you don't know who he is or where to find him?"

"I wasn't s'posed to see him. I kin write purty good, and all I had to do was write out what I heard and stick it under a certain rock he told me about, and the next night I'd find a ten dollar gold piece under it. Dang it, now I don't git the ten dollars!"

Ben had been thinking furiously. *Somebody hadn't been fooled*. Somewhere around town there was a suspicious mind who might upset the whole applecart and him with it. But *who*? The *Man*? Who else?

"That story's so damned outlandish I dang near believe it," Goodwin was saying. "You say you never seen this feller's face enough to know him if you seen him again?"

Selkirk shook his head. "Like I said, he never came into the light atall. Just stayed back in the shadders and talked."

"How'd he talk?" Ben asked. "Like a cowpoke—like a store clerk—like somebody with an edjucation?"

Selkirk squeezed water out of his sparse white hair as he thought. "Come to think about it," he said at last, "he didn't sound like no cowpoke, nor yet no store clerk. More like—" He stopped and appeared to cudgel his brain. "More like a—a—schoolteacher! That's it! Jist like my old teacher used to talk! You know—he didn't say ain't or cain't or none of the things like us ordinary folks use. Jist like a schoolteacher!"

Goodwin and Ben exchanged looks. "Tall or short, thin or fat?" Ben asked.

"Couldn't tell that, neither. Look—I'm givin' you the straight goods. You know, sheriff, that I git around plenty in my business, and there ain't but a few people in town and out of it I don't know. But I swear by the devil I ain't ever heard that man's voice before! If I was to hear it again I'd know it, though."

Ben nodded. "Chances are you'll get that chance." When Goodwin looked at him questioningly, Ben went on: "He wants to know about Mike Johnson, so we'll just fill his ear for him. Or his eyes, anyway. Selkirk, you're goin' to write him that note and collect your ten dollars."

A cracked grin spread over the old man's face. "I *am*?"

"You are. What did you hear us talkin' about?"

Selkirk thought a moment, his brow furrowed with the effort. "Why, about my booze, mostly, I reckon. But it ain't quite *that* bad. I ain't ever poisoned anybody yet."

"By inches, brother—by inches. So you heard us talkin' about your booze. Anythin' else?"

"Somethin' about has anybody left town or come in, but damned if I could make head or tail of that. Mebbe *he* could, but I couldn't."

Ben had taken off his shirt and was wringing out a sizable puddle in the dust of the yard. "Mebbe we can give him somethin' that'll interest him more than that. Let's see—sheriff, hadn't you left word for me to report to you the first time I was in town? And when I came here tonight didn't you warn me to keep my nose clean or you'd sling the key away on me? And didn't you tell me not to leave these parts till you had a chance to get answers to some letters you sent out—like you was tryin' to find out if I was wanted?"

"Whoa, now!" Goodwin complained. "Mebbe I *thought* some of them things, but I never—"

"The hell you didn't! I'm still shakin' from the dressin' down you gave me. And Harry, here, he heard it all. Didn't you, Harry?"

A crafty look had come into the old man's eyes and he let out a sudden cackle. "Mebbe I ketch on quicker'n the sheriff. He allus was the ploddin' type. So I write all that to this feller and say I stuck around till you left stompin' mad and Ace yelled after you not to forgit—he was keepin' his eye on you and you better walk light."

Ben slapped him on the shoulder and almost upset him. "Reckon you and me got to carry this thing off, if she goes at all. Seems like the sheriff—"

"Here, you wait, now!" Goodwin protested. "I kin play-act as good as anybody—you *know* that! Didn't I prove it that day in the saloon?"

"We-e-ll—" Ben hesitated just long enough to make Goodwin squirm a little more, "I reckon we can include you in. Right now, by God, I got to get my clothes dried out. You, too, old-timer. Anybody sees you and asks how you got wet, you tell 'em you was makin' a delivery and fell in the crick. Git, now, and you better not cross us or I'll look you up and make you swill down a quart of that stuff you make without takin' a breath."

Selkirk shivered with something more than wet clothing. "Man, if anythin' would make me tread the straight and narrer, that's *it!* Don't you worry none. That feller finds out what you told me, and nothin' else."

"All right." Ben looked at Goodwin, who nodded. "On your way. Sheriff, I'm goin' to have to set by your stove awhile till I dry off some."

They watched Selkirk scurry off out of the range of the oil lamp, and heard his hurried footsteps continue without a break. "Must see like a cat," Goodwin observed. "Stands to reason, though, since he's been a-prowlin' around after dark so damn long. Grab up an armload of that wood and we'll build up a fire for you."

Ben fortified his inner warmth with another jolt of Selkirk's masterpiece, and had just set the glass down when the sound of a shot rolled through the house.

"Six-gun," Goodwin said, making a dive for his own, which he had again hung over the chair.

"Nobody shootin' close to here," Ben said. "Well, looks like we better light a lantern and go look around."

Goodwin looked at him. "For what?"

The look Ben returned to him was one of strained patience. "Why, for old Selkirk's carcass, of course. It's my guess his friend wanted to see how square he'd be on his first trip, and follered him down here. Prob'ly hung around close enough to hear what went on and salivated Selkirk to let us know he was onto us."

Goodwin dug up a lantern with a chimney so dirty he had to scratch out an area for a narrow beam of light to shine through. "Gotta git around to cleanin' that one of these days," he muttered. He shuffled out the door with Ben close behind.

A half-hour later they found it—half stuffed under an overhanging rock by the creekside. Ben looked down at the face, which was not a pretty sight to see.

"Dead center," he commented. "His partner prob'ly stopped him for a palaver and damn near rammed the gun against his head when he let him have it. Gimme that lantern and keep your feet still. I'm goin' to look for a sign."

He found nothing but boot prints, which in the cattle country were a dime a dozen. There were no distinguishing marks in the prints. Ben moved slowly, back-tracking the prints for a distance of a hundred yards toward the road. Suddenly he stopped and raised his head, sniffing audibly.

He wet a forefinger and held it up, gauging the direction of the faint breeze. Finally he moved slowly to his right, bent far over to scan the ground. Goodwin almost craned his neck out of joint and then nearly fell over Ben when he stopped suddenly and picked up something.

Ben grunted with satisfaction. He held the stub of an expensive cheroot in the lantern light, then raised it for a good sniff. "Ain't many of these smoked around these parts, I'd say. Now, I ain't sayin' the party that puffed this thing is the one that shot ol' Selkirk, but I'd lay a small bet that if he hadn't been around here tonight the old-timer would still be livin'."

"Me too," Goodwin said. "Who the hell smokes them sissy things, anyways? Now lemme see." He went into deep thought for a moment, then shook his head. "Nope. Can't recollect anybody in particular. Might not be a bad idee to talk to the store man. He'd ought to remember who buys 'em."

"Good idee," Ben agreed. "Somethin' else. Did you notice anythin' about them boot tracks?"

"Can't say I did."

"The soles and heels both was new. Cut sharp, deep tracks. Now what damn cowpoke wears boots for more'n a day without runnin' them over at the heels and scuffin' the soles off on the outside?"

Goodwin thought, then bobbed his head vigorously.

"Then it's your idee this ain't no cowpoke we're lookin' for!"

"Nope. Not exactly. *But*, things *do* point to a feller in some other way of life. While you're askin' the store man about them seegars you might find out how many new pair of boots he's sold lately in—say size nine or ten. From what I been told, there ain't many cow people around here that can afford new boots."

"That's gospel! Well, reckon about the next thing is to go find my deppities and have them take ol' Selkirk in to the undertakin' room back of the livery stable. Durn it, somethin' allus comes up to spoil my evenin's. First you, then. . . ."

In a thick clump of bushes, a vague figure stirred as the two men began retracing their steps to the sheriff's cabin. There was a deep sigh of relief. *Let them talk to the storekeeper all they wanted.* He had bought both the boots and cheroots in a distant place. Anyway, he had what he wanted—first-hand, audible proof that Mike Johnson was not all he seemed, and maybe not even Mike Johnson. Just what he might be was still a mystery, but the very fact that he was on good terms with the sheriff spoke for itself.

A hunted man did not hobnob with his hunters, any more than a rabbit would play cozy with the hounds. He had not caught all that passed between the three men, but enough to find out that Selkirk meant to play the double-cross. This alone changed the picture of Mike Johnson as a wanted man. *And*, if he wasn't a wanted man, *what was he? Who was he? What was he looking for?*

A chill of alarm wiggled its way down the backbone of Harlow Bassett as he left his hiding place and hurried in a roundabout way toward town. He went to the rear entrance of the hotel in the alley, and just outside the door he took off the boots. With two quick motions he tossed them up on the flat roof of the building across the alley, then went into the entrance in sock feet.

Confident that his tracks were now covered, his confidence grew. *Mike Johnson, or whoever you are, you had better cover your tracks, too, or I'll find out just what breed of cat you are. Then, when they take you in, I can drop the roof on all your heads at once. See what that little hellcat has to say then about her unfailing judgment of men . . .*

The bottle had never felt more comforting nor the fire in it as cool and soothing. . . .

## CHAPTER 11

Ben Stratton, alias Mike Johnson, got drunk. Not play-acting drunk, but the kind of drunk that makes an ordinary man drool like an idiot, stumble around like a horse with the blind staggers, and talk in tongues.

It was for a purpose, and the purpose was so deeply ingrained in his conscious mind that a strong thread of it ran through his thoroughly drunken brain. He was going to find out who his friends were, if any, and perhaps those who did *not* wish him well. He had a sneaking hunch the latter would be in the majority, since he was a comparative stranger with the reputation of being a gunfighter and hence suspect.

He started out in the Drover, his clothes still damp from his ducking in the creek while capturing Selkirk. One of the bar-hangers looked curiously at the dark dampness of his shirt.

"Damn spooky hoss of mine," Ben grumbled sourly. "All I was doin' was takin' a nip out of a bottle crossin' the ford, and the damn fool must've seen a fish in the crick and thought it was gonna grab him by the hoof. Anyways, he throwed me star-high, and when I come down there was nothin' but a hell of a lot of water under me. Got soaked complete and had to lay out on the crick bank till I got dried off some."

The bar-fly grinned. "What happened to the bottle?"

Ben grinned back. "You can believe it or not, but I still had it in my fist when I got up. Didn't *di*-lute her hardly a-tall, either. Well, that's all water under the bridge, anyways. Mebbe some of this gent's firewater'll light a blaze in my innards and dry off my clothes the rest of the way. Have one?"

He made a fast friend right there—fast with a glass, that is. Ben looked with alarm at the way the set-out bottle grew lighter and emptier, and finally heaved a sigh of relief when the man's wife came and shrilled at him from the swinging doors. There was half a bottle left, and he grabbed it by the neck, picked out a table, and lurched over to it.

A dance-hall girl, all bangles and curled hair, came and

sat down. She gave him a painted, gap-toothed smile that almost cracked her face. "Hello, honey," she cooed in a whisky tenor. "Can I have a teensy-weensy little drink out of your bottle?"

"Gotta get your own glass," Ben mumbled thickly, a trick that was getting easier by the drink. "Ain't healthy to go drinkin' after other people. Doctor told me that. He'd ought to know. *He'd* drink after *anybody,* and he was the sickliest lookin' one man I ever laid eyes on."

She brought a glass from the bar and poured it full to the brim. "Here's to you, Mike Johnson, and may your bottle never get empty." Throwing back her head and dumping the glass at the same time, she performed the neatest bit of effortless swallowing Ben had ever seen. No gulping, just a silent slide down a gullet probably made of cast iron or turned to rawhide by practice in the art of getting rotgut whisky down without tasting it. *Empty bottle, here we come.*

"How'd you know who I am?" he asked.

She set the empty glass down and leaned forward on her bar-chapped elbows, showing a beefy expanse of chest that threatened to explode from her tight-laced bodice and cover the table a foot deep. "Who *don't* know you, honey? Everybody's been talkin' about the man that shot three road agents and sent Moss Finley back to his shop talkin' to himself. Where'd you come from, Mike Johnson, and where are you goin'?"

Ben made a vague gesture to the east, then to the west. "You name it, I been there or I'll be there b'fore I'm done. I've put hoss-prints in desert sand, mountain dirt, and Missouri mud. I've wallered in that big ol' salty thing they call the Pacific Ocean, boiled my brains out in Arizony, and I been up in them Grand *Tee*tons when I was damned glad I wasn't a brass monkey. Ma'am, you might say I'm either a well-traveled man or a saddle tramp. Most folks favor the latter."

She favored him with an understanding smile as she poured herself another brimming glassful. "I know how it is, honey. When I was just a little girl I wanted to travel so bad it hurt. That stinkin' farm had everything I didn't want—hogs to slop, chickens to feed, floors to scrub, clothes to wash—and I mean *dirty* clothes—plant cotton, chop cotton, pick cotton, haul cotton—Mike, I got so tired of cotton I ain't wore a goddam thing made o' cotton since I got enough money to buy anything else.

Looky." She proudly fingered the material of her chartreuse dress. "Silk. *Real* silk, and my stockin's are, too." She threw out her chest until Ben was ready to duck.

He stared at her owlishly. "How 'bout the rest of it?"

She cocked one eyebrow. "Rest of what?"

Ben waggled his fingers in an all-encompassing gesture. "The rest o' what you wear, dang it! Like drawers and undershirts and stuff like that. All that silk, too?"

She laughed uproariously, mopping her eyes with a handkerchief that sent waves of cheap perfume in a widening circle around her. "My Gawd, boy, where you been?" she finally gasped. "Just what you can see, honey—just what you can see."

"You mean you don't—" Ben shook his head sadly.

"You don't sling harness on a saddle horse," she said, went through the fascinating trick with the whisky, set the glass down, and belched genteelly behind her handkerchief, then fanned her flushed face with the bit of cloth. "My, it's hot in here!"

Ben focused his eyes on the perspiring face with an effort. "Sure is. Why don't you go outside and walk around awhile? I'll stay here and see nobody goes south with the bottle."

She looked at him archly. "Don't you want to come, too?"

He shook his head. "Me and night air don't get along. I caught the epizooticks once by breathin' night air, and I don't reckon I better take a chance."

Suddenly she was deadly serious. "Mike Johnson, I ain't askin' you to go for a walk with me to a damn room or anything like that. If you want to find out somethin' you ought to know, you better come along."

Ben's brain shoved back the effects of the last couple of drinks and evaluated the last remark. *Well, here's one, anyway. Takes someone that's seen the rough side to look out for the underdog. Maybe she knows somethin' I don't.*

Ben got to his feet and steered them in the general direction of the door. The blonde woman caught his arm and guided him to the batwings. "My name's Belle Ramsey," she whispered. "Act like a gay blade, dammit!"

Ben threw an arm around the ample waist and almost yanked her off balance. He threw back his head and gave out with a horrendous wolf howl that fairly made the skin crawl. "I'm a curly wolf and I'm a-lookin' for a howlin' partner! You willin' to do some plain and fancy howlin' with me, ma'am?"

"All right—all right, wolf-man," she humored him. "We'll go out and yell at the moon."

They went on through the swinging doors and turned right. At the first cross street, Belle pulled him off the main drag into the darkness. Fifty feet down the narrow side street the building ended, and Belle pulled him into the deeper shadows of an alley.

"All right, Mike Johnson," she said without preliminaries. *"If* you're Mike Johnson, that is—who wants your hide real bad in this town, besides Moss Finley?"

Ben was still fighting the foggy fumes that rose up and made hard work out of thinking. "Hell, I don't know. If I did, I wouldn't hesitate none to go and give the gent a chance to nail it to his barn door. I was hopin' someone might give *me* an earful—like you, mebbe?"

He felt her shrug in the darkness, her shoulder against his solar plexus. "Not much I can tell you, but I know someone that *might* be able to tell you a little more. He's a funny old coot—makes some God-awful booze out in the hills and peddles it around town to folks that will drink anything as long as it's cheap."

"Selkirk's dead." Ben shot it to her abruptly, and felt her stiffen against him. "Was he tellin' you about some gent wantin' him to keep an eye on me? Someone shot him."

There was an edge hard as a file in Belle's voice. "That poor little old thing. That little man that never hurt a soul in his life. Did you find out who did it?"

Ben pulled the cheroot butt from his pocket and held it under her nose. "Next time you smell one of these burnin' you might remember your little friend. Whoever did it left this along his back trail."

Belle sniffed deeply. "That ain't a new smell," she said slowly. "Of course, plenty of men in saloons smoke cigars and such to look important, but not stuff like this. This is *quality*, and I'm just the gal that can tell you that."

"That's what I thought." The night air was cutting the fuzziness from Ben's brain, and he knew how close he had come to getting too drunk to think straight, let alone act fast if the occasion demanded. He drew in deep breaths of the garbage-laden air from the alley. Mixed with Belle's perfume, it was enough either to clear a man's brain or his stomach.

Footsteps sounded on the hard-packed dirt of the side street and a hulking, shadowy figure went by.

"Moss Finley," Belle said when the man had gone. "Wonder what he's doin' out so late. They say he usually goes to bed with the chickens."

"Spyin' on that hash-slinger, mebbe," Ben said. "Anyways, he don't strike me as the type of man that'd put out good money for smokin' stuff like this. He's more of a Bull Durham man, seems to me."

"That's for sure. No, it wasn't Moss that shot Harry Selkirk. Harry told me about the man talkin' to him from the dark, but he'd of known if it was Moss. He sounds like a bullfrog croakin' at the bottom of a barrel."

Ben hesitated a moment, then said, "Belle, in your line of business—no offense meant, now—you meet up with a lot of people. I'd be obliged if you'd keep your sniffer goin' and let me know if you find anybody that smokes seegars like this."

She snorted. "Offense, hell! People like you and me don't need to beat around any mesquite bushes, Mike Johnson or whoever you are. Like you said, I meet up with a lot of people and get to smell a hell of a lot of breaths. If I get a whiff of this on anybody I'll let you know."

"You do that." Ben patted her shoulder.

At that moment a scuffling sound at the mouth of the alley alerted him, and with all his old reflexes working he shifted his big hand to the top of her shoulder and rammed her at full length down into the filth of the alley, sequinned dress and all. As he went down beside her, his gun was already leaping from its holster, and he twisted onto his side with the gun lined.

When the flash of the shot came at him, he had already taken up the slack of the trigger, and his answering shot was as close as an echo in a barn. He triggered two more fast ones, then leaped into a running crouch that sent him zig-zagging toward the attacker.

No gun flash jumped to meet him, no sound greeted him as he stopped, glued tight and thin to the rear of the building. He stayed that way for a full ten seconds, then cautiously stuck his head out, and looked around the corner. What he saw made him holster his gun and step out. The reflected light from the buildings across the main street had shown him the huddled figure, the six-gun that glinted five feet away from a limp hand.

Belle came out brushing off her dress and grumbling profanely. "Hell of a walk in the moonlight, I must say," was one of her milder remarks. "Who the hell you shot now, Mike Johnson?"

Ben was kneeling beside the man as footsteps approached cautiously from the main street. One man carried a lantern, very wisely at arm's length. When he saw that the action was over, he came to shine the light in the dead man's face. Then he grunted. "Allus knew that damn fool would come to no good end. Might as well talk to the wind."

"Who is he?" Ben asked. "He had a fair chance at me, but he was clumsy in the feet."

Belle leaned closer. "I know him. Name's Wes Ryan. Ain't seen him around town much lately, though."

"He s'prised us all and done went to work," another man put in. "That is, o'course, if you *call* that work. He's a'nursin' them white-faces of Carl Morris'."

Then Ben remembered why the dead face of the young man had rung a faint bell. He had seen him only once, from a distance, talking to Charlie Morris at the ranch, and they had taken turns looking at him as they talked.

## CHAPTER 12

The next day at the ranch, Ben managed to get his hat on and make some semblance of putting in a morning's work. Toby looked at him with a slow grin when they went to the corral for their horses.

"You look like you got kicked by a bottle last night," Toby commented.

Ben groaned. "Danged thing sneaked up behind me and popped its cork. Don't reckon you got a little bit of the hair of the dog in your bags?"

Toby shook his head, then turned as Carl Morris came up and spoke his name. "Better take Wes Ryan out with you this mornin', Toby. I want you to make a tally on that bunch over on the old Sylvester place."

Toby shrugged. "Ain't seen Wes this mornin'. Come to think of it, his bed ain't been slept in. Prob'ly made a night of it."

Ben held his tongue while Morris swore softly and

feelingly. "I gave that no-good a job against my better judgment, so I reckon I got no kick comin'. Well, grab off one of the other boys—one that can count over ten without takin' off his boots. Damn!" Morris turned and stalked off.

"What about this Ryan?" Ben asked.

"Just what Carl said—a no-good. I mean, no good for *anythin'*. Can't stick to a job more'n two weeks—can't play poker for beans, though he thinks he's a world beater—tried his hand at stealin' calves once and got caught first pop out of the box—did two years for that—and can't think like a cow. Just a plain no-good, and when he gits back Carl will tie the can to him so fast it'll make his head swim."

"Don't reckon that'll be necessary," Ben said matter-of-factly. "He ain't comin' back."

Toby shot him a look.

Ben shrugged. "Man goes tryin' to dry-gulch somebody in an alley he better shuck his boots or know how to get around without makin' a lot of noise. Like I said, he ain't comin' back."

"You?" Toby asked.

"Yep."

"Any special reason?"

Ben turned to look steadily as he could at the bewildered face, seeing that Toby was in fact surprised. "That's what I aim to find out. I never laid eyes on the gent till he was laid out last night, so he was put up to it by somebody else. Who that somebody else is, and why he wanted me amongst the daisies is about first on my list of things. You got any ideas?"

"Hell, no! I never took Wes for a dry-gulcher, even if he was a no-good. Only thing I can figger is somebody's got somethin' on him and *made* him do it. Otherwise he wouldn't have the guts to even shoot a man in the back."

Ben nodded. "Figgers. Next thing is—*who?* Anybody around here you can think of?"

Toby shook his head. "You ain't been around here long enough to make *that* kind of enemies. And, Wes didn't have no ambition to be a gunslinger that I know of, so he wasn't out to make a rep."

"Then I got to look for somebody that don't like me hardly none a-tall," Ben drawled. "Beats hell how a feller can come into a place peaceable-like and try to mind his own business, and have people try to beat him up, sling him in jail, dry-gulch him, and God knows what all. Makes a man feel like goin' over the hill."

Toby chuckled dryly. "Wouldn't be no different. Bet you had the same trouble everywhere you been. That's the trouble with bein' big—everybody wants to carve off a chunk so they won't feel so damn little."

"Reckon you're right there," Ben admitted. "Folks *do* seem to have a habit of scowlin' when they find out they got to look up to see my handsome face. Who you goin' to take out with us?"

Toby looked around, then beckoned to a young fellow with a pleasant face and lithe build. "Mike Johnson, Marty Engle. Reckon you'll ride with us today, Marty."

"Suits me." Engle shook hands with Ben, showing none of the usual surprise or resentment at his size. "How'd you like punchin' these fierce cows of ours?"

"Plumb terrifyin'," Ben said solemnly. "Dang near got laid on by one of the critters yesterday while I was off my horse layin' under a bush for a nap. Had to say boo twicet before she'd quit pesterin' me for bed room."

"Hear you durn near got laid on by an old bull in town, too," Marty said with a grin.

Ben nodded, then shook his head. "Can't figger Moss out, a-tall. How a man can claim a heifer before he slaps his brand on her is beyond me. Specially when the heifer's kickin' and squallin' that she don't want to run his range in the first place."

"Mebbe Moss sicked Wes on you," Toby suggested, and Marty shot him a questioning look. "Wes Ryan tried for Mike last night in the alley back of the saloon. We ain't got Wes no more."

Marty swore in mild surprise. "The danged fool! Not that it makes any difference now, but I could smell somethin' comin' up last night. Before he left for town he was spendin' a lot of time messin' with his gun, cleanin' it, and everythin'. I asked him, jokin'-like, if he was goin' huntin' coyotes. He looked at me sort of funny and said, 'Nope—skunks.' " Then Wes shook his head decisively. "You can forget about Moss, though. He'll stomp you, kick you, bite you, or anythin' else when he's fightin' you man to man, but he'd never sick a man with a gun on you."

Ben felt a great admiration for this youngster who could be so charitable toward the man who had almost beaten him to death. Moss *must* be a square shooter, or Marty Engle would likely be the last one to defend him. Somehow, Ben felt a great sense of relief at the revelation. He had formed a grudging respect for the bulldog tenacity of Moss in his stubborn quest for the hand of the fair Gloria, but damned if he didn't almost *like* the man now! He sighed, thinking that this wasn't the first time he'd probably have to fight again a man he'd formed a liking for. Ol' Moss was a ringtailed squealer, and you had to admire his stubbornness, if nothing else.

They rode all day tallying the herd of white-faces, and not once did Ben voice to Toby his suspicions that Charlie Morris was the man to look for. And, not once did Toby mention any such ideas on his own. Apparently he considered Charlie only as an ill-tempered, spoiled brat who needed his tail blistered with a length of whang-leather, but not as one who needed anything more serious.

When they rode back to the main ranch, the combination of warm sun and fresh breeze had pretty well erased the effects of the night before, and Ben was able to enjoy his burnt beef, beans, spuds, and biscuits. He walked out of the cookshack picking his teeth with a split matchstick and ran into Charlie just coming from the corral.

"Evenin'," Ben murmured around the toothpick, and Charlie stared at him as though he was a ghost. Ben nodded amiably, took out the toothpick, and spat a hole in the dust. "How was things up around the high country?"

"Why—uh—" Charlie was stuttering, his composure shattered for the moment.

Ben put the toothpick back and chewed it thoughtfully for a moment. "That's where you been, ain't it?"

"Why—uh—sure, but—" Charlie's dark, handsome face was a study in frustration. "Say, what the hell you drivin' at?"

Ben waved a lazy hand. "Nothin', brother—nothin'. Only, next time don't send a fumble-footed ama*choor* to do a perfessional's job. Now, you want me to go on and tell you what I'm drivin' at, or would you ruther I'd let it drop right here?"

Charlie muttered something and turned away, stomping toward the cookshack. Ben watched him part way, then walked to where Toby lounged against the watering trough, hunkered down on his heels. Ben hunkered down beside him.

"Now what was that all about?" Toby asked. "You and Charlie spittin' at each other again?"

"Nope."

"Looked like Charlie was mad enough to bite a railroad spike in two when he left."

"Yep."

Ben rolled himself a cigarette, lit it, and blew a dribble of smoke through his nose. "Bet Charlie chews spikes pretty easy," he guessed. "Don't strike me as the kind of man that takes things as they come."

Toby grunted, "Yep."

"Wants things all his own way. Other feller don't play the game his way, he picks up his marbles and goes home."

"Yep."

Ben turned to bend a quizzical glance on Toby. "Sounds like you done caught my fatal disease. Feller I caught it from finally died of lockjaw. Didn't open his mouth often enough to keep in the habit. Had to feed him with a straw through his nose for six months before he finally departed this mortal coil."

"Hah!" Toby found his voice again. "That ain't *about* to happen to you, the way you mopped up on the grub tonight! Every time you opened your mouth a whole danged biscuit disappeared, along with all the cow meat and beans you could stuff in the cracks. Don't talk to me about lockjaw. You got lockjaw about like one of them boy constrictors they tell about, that swallers a whole danged deer, horns and all!"

"Jealous, that's all. You people with the little bitty mouths and short arms is always jealous of people like me when it comes grub time. Not to change the subject—which I'm goin' to—when do I meet these people with all the gold and jools of the Orient they want to pour in my lap?"

Toby hesitated just a moment, then said, "I'll find out tomorrow. Let you know tomorrow night."

"Keno. Now let me tell *you* somethin'. I'll listen and I'll listen good—both ears—but if I don't like what I hear I'm goin' over that hill I was talkin' about, and nobody better try to stop me. That make sense to you?"

"Hell, yes! A man'd be a fool to buy a pig in a poke, and a bigger fool if he reached in without makin' damn sure he *had* a pig instead of a bobcat. You listen, that's all I ask, and you won't be lookin' for no hill."

Ben shifted around to mold his broad back more comfortably against the cool wood of the trough. "Tell you what. If money was gunpowder, I wouldn't have enough to blow the brains out of a flea. Now, this is a fine chance for these people to prove they're on the level with me. When you go to town tomorrow, you tell them that about a hundred big, round iron men'll go a long ways in draggin' me into the fold. I need britches, shirts, socks, and God knows what all."

Toby looked at him with a slow grin. "Hell, why didn't you say so?" He reached into the pocket of his Levi's and hauled out a roll of bills that would stop up a rainspout. He peeled off several bills and stuffed the rest back. "Here. If you need a hundred, mebbe two hundred'll be even more of a convincer. Pay me back when you draw your first share."

"Well!" Ben looked at the lovely sight lying in his hand, like succulent lettuce leaves lying on a calloused plate. "Looks like it pays off, all right. Funny how some of this stuff just layin' in a man's hand seems to warm him all over. All right. When you see these folks you can tell 'em they got a new boy."

"Good!" Then Toby was deadly serious. "First thing is to cover your tracks. When I go to town tomorrow you go with me. Draw your time first, tellin' Carl you decided to move on—itchy feet or somethin'—you can tell him whatever you want. Then when we go into town you go around to the saloon and let it out that you're leavin'."

"Brother, will I! And do you know the first one that's goin' to get a great, big goodby from me? That danged nosy sheriff, and if he bows his neck at me this time he ain't goin' to have to worry about the next election. Only reason I didn't dust off that long, skinny vest of his before was because I figgered I might settle here for awhile."

"Leave the sheriff alone!" Toby said sharply, and when Ben looked at him with an amiable challenge, "What I mean is, *this* sheriff is worth a hell of a lot more to us alive than dead. Long as he's in office we know he ain't goin' to bust his neck tryin' to run us down, while somebody else *might.*"

"Hm-m." Ben nodded slowly. "I can see where you're right, so I won't pick on him none. Just want to let him know he didn't have me buffaloed. What else?"

"When you leave, head west and keep goin' till you run clean out of the valley and hit the foothills. Up on the second hill where the road's steepest just before it goes over the top, you'll see an old Injun trail leadin' off to the north. You can tell it by the old dead oak tree right where it leaves the road."

"That road traveled much?"

Toby shook his head. "You might see a few people, no more. You turn on the trail and ride about five miles to where it goes through a narrow gap between two big rocks. You can't miss *that*. A long time ago someone painted on one of the rocks—'Prepare for the end of the world.' "

"Sounds real appetizin'," Ben mused. "Mebbe that's exactly what I'll be doin'."

Toby was matter-of-fact. "You go about things wrong, that's about right. Anyways, there'll be someone waitin' for you there at the gap. It'll be either Slim Parker or Gilly Gahagan. From there on, someone'll be with you all the time."

"From there on to where?"

Toby smiled slowly. "Mister, from there on, there are so many trails criss-crossin' that a stranger could lose hisself complete inside of a mile's ride. And you know, the funny thing about them trails is they don't go *nowhere.*"

Ben grinned in return. "I get it. If they take a feller in there and find out they don't want him, they could just turn him loose and let him starve to death tryin' to find his way out."

Toby shook his head. "They find somethin' wrong, he usually ain't got time to starve to death. What I'm tryin' to tell you is, a man'd better be damn sure of hisself *before* he goes in there, if he ever figgers on comin' out."

Ben sighed. "Well, I don't reckon it's any dangerouser than ridin' around the country just mindin' your own business. *That's* how *I* get in trouble. Somebody always pokes his nose up agin mine and snorts, or pulls a gun on me because he sees a nice big target, or some damn rannyhan of a sheriff's got too much empty room in his jail."

Toby motioned slightly with a thumb, and Ben saw Charlie Morris glaring at him as he left the cookshack and started toward the house. "Reckon I kinda stirred him up a little bit," Ben said. "Bet he's wonderin' just what I meant about that Ryan feller. Never told him how it wound up."

"Let him guess till he finds out," Toby said. "He'll find out when he goes into town, anyway, prob'ly tonight."

"And me, I'll be in town tomorrow and likely have to answer a lot of damn fool questions that sheriff'll throw at me about last night. Lucky that dancin' gal was with me and can tell him Ryan tried to dry-gulch me."

Toby nodded. "And you better take it easy on how you ruffle his feathers or you might be hangin' around there for a long time waitin' to get cleared of that killin'. He can make it mighty tough on you."

"Reckon you're right. I'll be all sugar and spice with him, much as it goes agin my grain. Well, reckon I'll go in the bunkhouse and ketch up on some of them old newspapers. Even old news is new news if you ain't seen it before."

Charlie came from the house wearing a clean outfit of town clothes, passing Ben on his way to the bunkhouse. He glared his dislike of the bigger man. "I've just talked to my father," he said shortly. "Tomorrow you go up the hill and work with the regulars."

Ben gave him an easy smirk. "Sonny, you done put your oar in with your pappy just a mite too late. Tomorrow mornin' I start makin' big tracks out Californy way. These white-faces sorta got me used to easy livin' and I don't want to get out of the habit. Give my regards to the ol' mossyhorns and kick 'em in the ribs a couple of times for me."

Charlie's look was pure hatred for a long moment before he turned on his heel and strode away.

## CHAPTER 13

Gloria Lambert had sold her product well. The fact that Mike Johnson was a wanted man, proven by the circular Toby had found in his saddlebags, had completed the deal as far as Hugh Andrews was concerned. In addition to that, he had come to have implicit faith in Glory's ability to read people and pick nothing but winners.

Take that Harlow Bassett, for instance. On his own initiative, Andrews wouldn't have given Bassett more than a passing glance, and a contemptuous one, at that. But Glory had insisted, and to his surprise Bassett had proven to be a most valuable asset to the organization.

He seemed to have a nose for news of cattle concentrations and shipments, seeming always to be in the right place at the right time. The information he had delivered had resulted in easy work and big pay, and with his city slicker manner and innocent front he seemed destined just to continue on and on.

Andrews set down his glass of wine and ran slender fingers through his thick, iron-gray hair. A small smile touched his slightly petulant mouth as the usual thought struck him. The thought was actually a form of self-questioning—what would the good people of the town and the country around think if they knew their respected *schoolteacher* was in reality the mastermind of the Black Butte gang? It was a question that never failed to excite him, that *he,* considered by most to be small, insignificant, and sadly lacking in the stuff men are made of, should be the one whose brains were making virtual paupers of many cattlemen who had looked down their noses at him, and whose strategy had made fools out of those who had tried to break up the gang.

True, there *had* been tight moments, like when the detective from the Cattlemen's Association had taken a posse far into the buttes and actually fought their way clear to the stronghold. But that trying moment, like all the other lesser ones, had been resolved favorably. The detective—let's see—Frank Chambers was his name—had been taken alive and was still being held as an ace in the hole. He would make a valuable hostage in case any group mounted a massive attack.

This Mike Johnson must be quite a man, to inspire such superlatives from Glory. Still, an *enigma.* A big man—impressive as to size, personality, and ability—yet dressing and acting like a saddle tramp. On the other hand, this man might be an expert in playing them close to the vest. A wanted man could certainly conceal his identity more successfully as a member of the lowest strata than he could in any other way.

Andrews sighed and picked up his glass. He held it up to the last rays of the sun shafting in through the window, seeing in its glowing depths the bright promise of his future. A future, his mind exulted, that would hold no tolerant smiles—no penurious school board doling out dollars that were squeezed out of shape—no runny-nosed brats droning out lessons with complete ignorance of their meanings—and above all, no more—*never, by God*, a forced respectability and fawning subservience to a damned community who considered him merely a cog in a machine designed to cram education into the doltish minds of their offspring like a sausage stuffer fattens a hog gut.

No more of that. Instead, there would be the fine cities of the world and all they had to offer. Fine food—fine wines—the theater and other forms of entertainment for the discerning man. The adulation that naturally comes to those with money, *and money he would have!*

Already, in his secret hiding place in the cellar of the school building, there was a heavy leather bag containing over a hundred thousand dollars in currency—all good as the gold that was too heavy to maneuver. One hundred thousand reasons why he was able to sit in the growing darkness and chuckle. And, one hundred thousand reasons why the world was assuming more and more the aspects of an oyster—*his* oyster to open with the magic wand of wealth, and eat its meat at his leisure.

But *alone?* Unthinkable, after all these years of sterile existence, that he should continue a life of denial and pseudo-respectability. *Gloria.* Ah, there was a one! He had steeled himself against any show of emotion toward her for a very good reason. Bring a woman up to your level, or drop yourself down to hers, and you are no longer a whole man. No longer do you alone make the decisions, and if you're not careful you find yourself taking orders instead of giving them.

No, thank you. The fiery shoots of color in the glass he held up had dimmed to a dull glow, but the beauty was still there for the discerning man to see. Still there like the dormant pleasures awaiting him, ready to burst into life at the first rays of a new day. He sipped from the glass and then suddenly tossed the entire contents down his throat in one glorious swallow.

And *that* would be the way he would take life—in huge, satisfying gulps, chewing it over only when the taste should dictate. *Gloria!*

With her on his arm, the Louvre would be his alone, and the Champs Eylsées his personal boulevard. The Alps would be no higher than foothills, and the deepest ocean a mere pond. *That* was a woman to stir a man to his depths. He decided to speak of it to her tonight, when they had a meeting slated at her sister's. Then—the one big *last* job, and after that the far places and the dream to be lived! . . .

Once again Glory Lambert and Harlow Bassett made the trip from Longhorn to Rockport in the light rig. And once more Glory brusquely ordered Bassett to stay in his hotel room in case Hugh Andrews wanted to see him. And, just as naturally, he was consumed with rage at being ordered around by her.

Tempering his rage with caution, however, he made no mention of his suspicions of Mike Johnson. Instead, he went into the hotel in seething silence, and left his room only long enough to buy a bottle. Then, with the contents of the bottle oiling his brain and reflexes, he practiced for a full hour with his six-gun.

Strange, how practice would make a man's fingers and thumb seem to have brains of their own, independent of the nerve center that controlled the more mundane actions. All that center had to do now was to give the command, and the hand swept back in a precise curve that furled the coattail away from the high-riding holster in one smooth, free-flowing motion. Then, at the end of its sweep, the hand would become a living entity.

Palm would slap butt, fingers curl, thumb hook, trigger finger poise and trip trigger; all in the time it took for his *other* hand to slap at a mosquito. Bassett felt a sense of security he had never known before. In a land of violent men he had found violence in himself, and the means to justify its existence.

Even the horrible suit took on less and less significance. The knowledge that he could avenge any slur on his appearance or put out a sly wink with a bullet made him feel almost jovial toward the world. He had all he could do to keep from going down to the saloon. This feeling of equality with *any* man should be exhibited, not hidden under a bushel.

But he remembered that Hugh Andrews just *might* send for him, and he wanted to be ready for that, above all. For the first time since their initial meeting, he would show Andrews *not* a subservient underling, eager to please, but a poised, sure man of the world who knew his worth and expected to be totally recompensed for it. Then, if Andrews got on his high horse, or tried to talk him out of the larger share he intended to demand . . . After all, there were other places for a man of talents who could use either his tongue or his gun with equal facility. And if he was driven to that, he would do so with the satisfaction of having deprived the Black Butte gang of their leader. To put it simply, he told himself, Hugh Andrews was treading a very narrow path, and the direction in which he veered would tell if he lived or died.

Bassett took another healthy swig from his bottle and put the gun back in his valise. He had not worn the gun in public as yet, preferring to keep it as a surprise when a surprise was indicated. The only other use it had was when he was in lonely places on his rounds of the ranches and towns.

Then he would drive off into some secluded spot, set up rocks, chunks of wood, or some bottles he had collected or saved, and combine his drawing with target practice. In the four months he had owned the gun, he had progressed from a rank beginner to a really dangerous man with a gun, all the more dangerous because he was an unknown quantity.

Bassett raised the window shade and opened the window. He stood in the opening and breathed deeply of the clean evening air. A deep nostalgia welled up in him. These were alien sounds and smells, the hallmark of the hick, the breath of the one-horse town, the one-store, two-saloon burg.

Give him the clang of the horse-car bells, the click of heels on pavement instead of the hollow thud of boots on boadwalks. *Take me back to the land of the big river, where steamboats moan by on the muddy flood and a man can stand on any street corner and see dozens like himself—where boots and tight pants are an exception rather than the rule, and where the paint you see isn't all on barns.*

All evening he waited, and no knock came on his door. A snub. A distinct snub from the man whose pockets he had lined with money, and from the woman who had been all sugar and spice until she had him hooked. What had she said—? *After you hook the fish it's foolish to feed it more bait . . .*

Bassett took one more deep swig out of the bottle before turning in. In spite of having drunk half of the quart of high-proof whisky, he felt cold sober. He went to sleep without a backward thought, having already laid out his course of action. Hugh Andrews would come across or die.

## CHAPTER 14

Early the next morning, Ben Stratton went to the house to see Carl Morris. Morris' wintry eyes surveyed him closely when Ben asked for his time. "Charlie been botherin' you, or any of the other boys?" he asked.

Ben shook his head. "Nope. Ain't many people bother me. It's only that I got the itchy heel again. Damn good thing I ain't a chicken. Wouldn't set still long enough to lay an egg."

Morris shrugged. "If that's the way you want it. I sort of hoped you'd stay on for awhile till my man gets back on his feet. Puts me in a real bind, with Charlie goin' away and all."

"Goin' away?" Ben asked.

"I'm sendin' him to see the army commander at Denver. Try to sell 'em good beef soon's I'm ready to ship some of the white-faces. They been buyin' regular stuff from me."

"You ain't gonna sell that army no *high-priced* beef," Ben told him. "Somebody's got to make a profit on stuff like beef, and it ain't gonna be *you.*"

"They've treated me all right," Morris said stiffly.

Ben nodded. "Sure. Go ahead. Only, I reckon you been in the cow business long enough to have an understandin' with the buyer *first.*"

He rolled up his bed, caught up his horse and loaded him, and rode off without a backward glance. He had spoken to Toby only once, briefly. Toby said only, "You're in," and went on with his breakfast. That was the last word that passed between them. Now, Ben pulled his horse off the road into a clump of brush and waited for Toby to catch up with him.

Toby came along in a few minutes, and they continued on toward town together. Ben could not help but feel a deep regret that this likable youngster was one of the enemy, a self-confessed rustler and likely also a killer.

"How'd you happen to get in this game?" Ben asked.

Toby grinned. "Ambition, mebbe. I been poor all my life, and damned if I could ever form a likin' for it. What I want is enough money to buy a nice little spread, marry me a red-cheeked gal, and spend the rest of my life raisin' kids and cows. Workin' for wages, all hell'd freeze over before I'd git *that* kind of money. Anyways, when somebody asked me how I'd like to make some *easy* money, and lots of it, I snatched it quick."

"Sorta risky, though, here where people know you."

"Huh-uh. It's been the other way around. Long as I keep my two jobs separated and don't try to let 'em overlap, I'm safer than if I was a stranger. Like you."

Ben grunted. "Yeah—like me. All I got to do is stick my nose in a town and somebody tries to give me an extry nose-hole with a six-shooter. Hah! Just wait till I tell that sheriff I'm movin' on! He'll have a mess of kittens right there on his desk!"

Toby turned in his saddle to face him. "Better not tell him anythin'. You go spoutin' to him, he's liable to hold you for that killin' the other night, like I told you. Don't forgit the other time you was in that *calabozo* of his. Bet you still got scratch marks on your pelt."

Ben scratched vigorously at the memory: "Hell, I got scratch marks on my backbone where I scratched clean through from my belly! Glad you mentioned that. Reckon I better swaller my pride and just tell him bye-bye."

"Why tell him anythin'?"

Ben shook his head. "First place, he done told me not to leave town without tellin' him. Can't do no more'n be courteous to a nice cuss like him, can I?"

"Just be careful *what* you say. You git yourself in real trouble with the sheriff, these folks is liable to take a second think about you and mebbe decide you ain't worth the risk."

Ben rubbed his chin. "*That* won't do, at all. Not when I got all that money half spent already. Dang it, looks like I got to be nice to that stringbean even if it chokes me."

They were riding past Moss Finley's saddle shop when the door opened and Moss rolled out onto the boardwalk. "Hey, you!" Moss rumbled, pointing a sausage-sized finger at Ben.

Ben pulled his horse around abruptly and got off. He took off his gunbelt, hung it over the saddle horn, then walked up in front of Moss, hitching up his pants. "Hey, yourself," he said, his brows drawn down. "Mister, you done stuck your voice in my ear at the wrong time. In the few days I been in or near this danged town I been waylaid, slung in jail, et up by bugs, dry-gulched in an alley and bruised up my kncukles on that thick head of yours. Now, by thunder, I aim to take *all* that out on you, so git them damn meat-hooks up!"

Moss took a short step backward and held up a hand. "Whoa up a minute, now! I didn't come out here to fight you."

Ben stopped, suspicious, his fists cocked. "You didn't?"

Moss shook his shaggy head. "Reckon there's a hell of a lot of folks I fought that I shouldn't of. Seems like sometimes a feller gits somethin' in his head and can't git it out with a crowbar."

Ben lowered his hands. "You mean like that hash-slinger?"

Moss nodded. "Found out she didn't care a damn about me—just wanted to see me beat fellers up, I reckon." He stopped for a moment, shook his head, then went on, wonderment in his gravelly voice. "Funny, how a pretty little thing like that kin be so damn bloodthirsty!"

"Hah!" Ben snorted. "You don't know the half of it, brother! She likely clapped her little hands when I mashed that beezer of *yours*, too. Leastways, she *asked* me to stomp you real good."

Moss groaned. "And to think I done give her the best fights of my life! Well, the hell with her from now on. I'll do my fightin' in the saloons, like a self-respectin' gent ought to. Fellers, will you jine me in a drink and let *me* make the toast?" He held out a hairy paw and Ben grasped it.

Jaws dropped all up and down the street and unbelieving murmurs broke out as Moss was seen to shake hands with the man who had publicly whipped him. Eyes popped when they beheld the man they knew as Mike Johnson lay a friendly hand on Moss Finley's brawny arm and propel him to the nearest set of swinging doors.

The barkeep took one look to see what had darkened the doorway so effectively, then reached under the bar and brought out a sawed-off shotgun with trembling hands.

"G-gents," he stuttered, "I'm scared as hell, but I'll be d-damned if I'll stand by and watch you wreck the place. You do your fightin' outside, like you did last time!"

Ben, Moss, and Toby bellied up to the bar, disregarding the waving muzzle of the greener. "Have faith in your fellow-man," Ben said solemnly, "and while you're at it kindly aim that widow-maker the other way. Whisky, and if I ketch you sneakin' out to the livery stable for it you better have the sight filed off of that weepon."

The bartender hesitantly lowered the shotgun. "You mean you fellers buried the hatchet?"

Moss glowered at him. "Dang it, if we'd of come in here to fight, the roof would be fallin' in already. We come to drink, and by God if you don't trot it out pronto there's another saloon right close by!"

The bartender grinned and wiped his sleeve on his perspiring brow as he shoved the shotgun back under the bar. "Best in the house," he promised. "This is the dangdest thing I ever seen! Mind tellin' me what God hath wrought with you two?"

"We seen the error of our ways," Ben said. "We done decided that peace and harmony is easier on the face and hands. Your gonna pour that snake pizen or just nurse the bottle?"

Moss watched the pouring morosely, then engulfed a glass in his hamlike hand. "Cuss the women," he announced, and downed the liquor. Ben and Toby followed suit. They had two more quick ones while they added their uncomplimentary sentiments regarding the fair sex.

"What in thunder's got you three so upset over women?" the bartender asked. "If I was to get drunk every time a woman's made a idiot out of me I'd never draw a sober breath. Somebody just ain't acquainted you gents with the facts of life."

"Such as what?" Moss growled.

"Such as why a man that's supposed to have good sense will let a little bitty woman scramble his brains till he can't hit his rump with both hands. Only one way to handle them, take it from me. Wine 'em, dine 'em, love 'em, and leave 'em, in that order."

"Hah!" Moss exploded. "With that there woman, you don't do *none* of them things, in no order! Used to give me winks and little nudges when she set down my plate and that was *all*. And now I know why, by hell. She knowed I'd slap the socks off'n anybody that looked at her after that, and that's what she wanted. I wasn't nothin' but a dang fightin' machine for her to play with. Wish *she* was a man for about three minutes!"

He downed his fifth whisky in two minutes, then turned to stare owlishly at Ben. "Wanna fight just for fun? No hard feelin's or nothin'? Just to see if you kin do it again?"

Ben shook his head. "I might not be so lucky next time. Besides, I'm pullin' out for the faraway places, and I don't want to look any worse than I have to when I meet strange people."

"Aw, you can't do that!" Moss protested. "You and me kin have a lot of fun together! Ever' so often we git a few Texas boys comin' through here and there ain't nothin' they like better'n a good fight. Some of the fellers around here, too, long as you take 'em two at a time."

"Nope. I already done told my horse we was leavin', and I can't go back on my word. Reckon I'll take a stroll around and tell some of the folks so long. I'll likely see you before I pull out, Toby."

Toby nodded and raised a forefinger. "Better do like I said and not make that sheriff mad at you."

"Sheriff?" Moss rumbled, hitching up his pants over his ample belly. "That rannyhan givin' you trouble? By God, I'll go over there and stick my foot in his mouth, grab him by the ears, and yank him on like a boot! Can't make trouble for *my* friends, by Granny! You just say the word—"

"Nothin' like that," Ben soothed him. "It's just that he might want me to hang around till they clear up that business the other night."

"Clear up, my eye! That's cleared up and then some. Belle done told me. That Ryan feller was goin' around tellin' a few folks about how he was aimin' to stop your clock. If that don't make it self-defense I'll eat your—" He stopped and took a closer look at Ben's shapeless, messy hat. "Nope, not *that* one, but I'd eat a *clean* hat if they could hold you *ten minutes* for gunnin' down that damn bushwhacker. First place, it's only been a question of time when that Ryan'd git lead poisonin' in his gizzard."

"Glad to hear *that*," Ben said. "Reckon I better go see him, anyways, just to keep the record clear." He fished out the money Morris had paid him and peeled off a bill, prudently keeping the roll Toby had loaned him under cover. "You gents go ahead and do battle with that bottle, and I'll try to git back before you play taps over it."

He walked to the batwings, shoved them open, and stepped to the boardwalk. He sniffed deeply of the fresh air to get the saloon out of his lungs, then froze in his tracks. From somewhere, carried on some vagrant breeze, had come a remembered smell, one that had become imprinted on his senses until there would be no mistake

It was the rich smell of expensive tobacco, the same that had filled his nostrils the night he stood seething with impotent rage as he sniffed the cheroot butt dropped by the cold-blooded killer of a harmless old man. . . .

## CHAPTER 15

Ben found Goodwin sitting behind his desk, his feet propped up on its once polished surface. "Seems to me you're pretty danged careless with that desk top, after you raised so much hell with me for scarrin' it up."

Goodwin's long face showed little humor. "Once a hoss has a broke leg, ain't no use tryin' to ride him careful."

"Any luck spottin' that gent that smokes them expensive seegars?" Ben asked after filling him in on events.

Goodwin shook his head.

"Got a whiff of it a few minutes ago," Ben said. "I walked around for awhile but couldn't make out where it was comin' from. Now look. And for God's sake, *listen.* Today I pull out to join up with the Black Butte Gang."

Goodwin's feet hit the floor with a jarring thump. "You're *what?* You gone out of your mind, man?"

Ben hunkered down against the wall and began to build a cigarette. "What better way do you know to find out things? You want to count how many horses there are in a barn and see what color they are, you don't stand off and take a squint at the outside with a spyglass. You git inside. I aim to find out how many mavericks they got runnin' loose in them hills."

Goodwin mopped his suddenly perspiring brow. "Well, you're pickin' the surest damn way I know to commit suicide. You think for a minute there ain't some brains *in* them hills, too, as well as the one that runs them from somewhere out here? You'll slip somewhere, and when you do—"

Ben calmly lit his smoke before speaking. "Goodwin, I set this thing up just that way, and that's the way it's goin' to be played. I saddle-tramped it in here with a planted wanted dodger in my saddlebags just in case some curious gent got to prowlin' through them. Them three long-loopers outside of town was a godsend, and ol' Moss didn't hurt any, either."

Goodwin grunted. "You fall in a hawg-pen, you'd waller out with a fistful of rubies. You needed somethin' to make you out a tough feller, and it all fell in your lap. All right—say you jine up with them. *Then* what happens? You capture them all single-handed, mebbe?"

Ben grinned. "My mother raised some foolish young'uns, but no out-and-out *crazy* ones. What would you say if I told you that *one telegram would send two hundred men into the Black Buttes within eight hours?"*

The sheriff's jaw dropped. "You're foolin'!"

Ben shook his head. "I *told* you there was a lot of hard feelin's about Frank Chambers disappearin' the way he did. The Association don't take kindly to havin' its men wiped out like so many coyotes. Neither does the Federal Marshal's office. That's why I'm here, and that's why you'll send a telegram to Hooker in Abilene."

"He's head man?"

"The top. Then he'll contact our men out here and set it up."

Goodwin was shaking his head unbelievingly. "I still can't see where the hell he'd git two hundred men out here! You couldn't find that many men you could trust!"

Ben got up, stretched, and ground out his cigarette in the tin can on the desk. "We didn't git them here. They was brought in."

Goodwin shook his head in wonderment. "Man, when you people do a thing you do it up brown, don't you? Who are they?"

"The damndest bunch of fightin' men, pound for pound, in the whole country. Mixture of old soldiers from one side or the other, and some tough old mountain men throwed in. Hooker manages to keep 'em busy enough to stick together most of the time. Other times they hire out to—well, other outfits."

"I'll be damned! But, that many men'd be bound to make somebody suspicious, all in one bunch."

Ben grinned and shook his head. "Over at Woodbury, just outside of town, there's a big land clearin' job goin' on. Just by some coincidence, there's two hundred men workin' on it. And settin' on a sidin' in the Woodbury yards there's twenty-five boxcars that ain't goin' nowhere till a telegram gits sent."

"Then what?"

"Then the railroad hooks them cars onto an engine and hauls them through the valley to the point closest to that trail. There's where the men and horses will wait for my okay. All them boys want is excitement."

"Besides the telegram," Ben went on, "there's somethin' else. You'll have to put three men *you* can trust on a job."

"I got 'em," Goodwin said promptly. "What's the job?"

"A day and night watch on the highest hill between here and the Buttes. Nighttime, I'd signal with a fire. Smoke signals in the daytime."

"How'll they know what you're sayin'?"

"Jim Manley, the man in charge of the two hundred, knows the code, and I'll leave you a copy of it. Your men will have to write down what they see so there'll be *no mistake*. We don't want to throw away another bunch of lives through mixed-up reports. They'll have to keep a sharp watch. I don't know that country, and I'll just have to send the signals from the nearest high point."

He took pen and paper and made a copy of the code for Goodwin, who folded it carefully and stowed it in a shirt pocket, buttoning it in securely.

Goodwin shook his head. "I still don't like the idee of you goin' in there alone."

Ben shrugged. "No other way I *could* git in. My invitation don't include any guests."

"I know—I know. But I don't like it." He shook his head. "Toby. Allus liked that young feller. Reckon he got a taste of easy money and liked it. Any idee who some of the others might be?"

"None at all. All I know is Toby saw them last night, so they got to be around close. How come you've been sheriff here for God knows how long and don't know any more'n you do about your people?"

Goodwin's long face grew longer. "The *last* one to know anythin' like that is the sheriff, and you know it. A man kin beat his wife, kick his mother-in-law, or snore in church, and everybody from the shoeshine boy to the banker knows about it—but the sheriff? Hah!"

"You ought to git out and dig around more. I'll tell you one thing. When the bunch starts into the Buttes, I want you to be right along with them."

Goodwin bristled. "What gives you the idee I wouldn't be of my own accord? Only reason I ain't cleaned that gang out already is because I didn't have the men! Man, with *two hundred* it's just about a cinch."

"Cinch or not, I got to get somethin' to eat before I pull out. Now remember the trail I'm to take—leaves the road on top of the second hill by the old dead oak."

"Got it. Will this Jim Manley know it?"

Ben shook his head. "You'll tell him. *And,* you'll be guidin' part of the bunch in the way you went, so the whole shebang can't be dry-gulched."

Goodwin's chest swelled a trifle. "I'll take 'em in, boy, and bring 'em out or my name ain't Ace Goodwin."

"You bring 'em out or your name's mud," Ben told him flatly. "This is one time you ain't goin' to peek behind a few bushes and then hightail it for home."

Goodwin puffed up with indignation. "Now you look here, boy! You and me's been pretty friendly up to now, but—"

"We ain't been friendly," Ben cut him off. "We just been gettin' along is all. And we'll keep on gettin' along if you hold up your end. Now I'm gonna snatch that grub and be on my way. And remember to git them watchers out on the hill soon as you can. I might decide to smoke the sky up any time."

Ben left the office and walked toward the restaurant. Toby was lounging against the front of the hotel, and fell into step beside him. "How'd you make out with the stringbean?"

Ben grunted. "Just about what you'd figger. Gave me a lecture about how crime didn't pay and I'd be better off to shuck my gun and take on a steady job with some good cow outfit and how good-hearted he was not to hold me for trial for killin' that damn Ryan."

Toby chuckled. "With election comin' up before long you're lucky to git off this easy. All you got now is a earache, when you *could* be collectin' another flock of bug bites."

Ben shuddered. Creepy, crawly things that a man couldn't get in the sights of a gun or put a boot-heel on always gave him the jim-jams. He was glad there was no more reason for him to spend any additional time in Goodwin's pokey.

Glory Lambert smiled at them from behind the counter. "Hi, you two! What are you doing in town so early in the day?"

Toby gestured at Ben. "This danged fool done went and quit his job. I tried to talk him out of it, but you might as well try to stop a duck from goin' south."

Glory looked at Ben with wide eyes. "Why, you can't do that, Mike! We've just gotten to know you, and now you want to move on and never see us again! Why don't you stay?"

Ben shrugged. "Aw, like I told Toby, I git the itchy foot and nothin'll scratch it but walkin' on strange land. Somethin' I can't help, I reckon, like a man bein' born with blue eyes or crooked teeth. Speakin' of teeth, you look like you been bitin' an oyster and done stole his pearls."

She tinkled him a laugh. "That's about the nicest thing that's ever been said to me. Toby, why didn't you tell me he was a poet?"

"Bet he can't rhyme cat and rat," Toby said. "Speakin' of oysters, I see you got oyster stew on the me-and-you. Trot some out, and I'll see if I can't git me a pearl first-hand."

"Double that order," Ben said. When she went toward the kitchen, he glanced idly around the restaurant. His eye fell on a man in an atrocious suit of loud checks, topped by a derby hat of a bilious green hue. Yellow shoes gleamed below the tight-cuffed pants. To himself, Ben said *whew!* Here was one of the kind you read about but seldom see. Must've escaped from some travelin' road show or a circus side show.

Then Ben's eyes traveled to the eyes regarding him from beneath the derby rim and his casual, amused inspection ceased. *For some reason, the stare being bent on him was one of pure hatred!* As he looked, the eyes shifted from him to the man's plate as he resumed eating.

Ben oozed over slightly on his stool toward Toby. "Don't look now," he said in an undertone, "but who's the comic valentine over yonder?"

Toby chuckled softly. "That, my friend, is one of your feller-workers." Then, as Ben gasped, "S'prised? Can't say I blame you. Fact is, though, this Bassett's one of the best herd scouts you can *ee*magine. No cowman would take him for anythin' but a harmless city feller, and he rides all over hell and gone in that buggy of his pin-pointin' cow-people for us. Works real good."

"Bassett?"

"Harlow Bassett. S'posed to be sellin' crazy canned stuff to the ranchers—you know—pickled hummin'birds' tongues, boiled quail livers, sautéed mosquitos' eyebrows —stuff like that."

Ben's eyebrows shot up. "Crazy is *right!* You can't sell stuff like that to people that's used to burnt cow and bacon and beans."

Toby chuckled again. "That's the point. Who'd expect a feller like that to be lookin' over herds to see which ones would be the easiest to steal? I'll tell you, the boss has a head on his shoulders."

Ben pricked up his ears. *His* shoulders. Well, that narrowed it down a bit, anyway. It *was* a man that ran the shebang. Ben reflected that some folks might think him crazy for having suspected it might be a woman, but that was only because they'd never met or heard of ol' Ma Pickett, back in Texas, who ran a hardcase crew with an iron hand and stole everything that wasn't nailed down. Got away with it for ten years, too, till she got too big for the man's britches she wore and had her boys make off with the proceeds of a big cattle drive. That got all the people down on her at once, and they proceeded to end her business operations with a few hundred feet of rope, thereby making her the only woman in that section to do an aerial *fandango.*

Glory brought their oyster stew and stood listening to the juicy duet as they dug into it. After the third spoonful, Ben looked up to see her regarding him quizzically. "Mike Johnson, you're a fraud. Why don't you break down and tell me what you *are* going to do—*truthfully?* Or would you rather I told you?"

Ben shot a look at Toby, who merely kept on spooning oyster stew into his mouth. "Why, I told you," he said, puzzled. "I aim to see what's over the hill."

She leaned her soft, rounded elbows on the counter and brought her face closer to his. "No, you're not, Mike. You're going to the old blasted tree on the second hill and turn to the right. You're going to ride for maybe an hour and then you'll be met at the Slot and—"

Ben let his feet drop to the floor from the footrest and shoved himself back from the counter, looking at Toby accusingly. "Now just what in the hell is this! I risk my neck to listen to you and go in on a deal, thinkin' you people had enough sense to keep your mouths shut, and now, by God, I find out that even the town hash-slingers know all about it! Well, you can count me out if that's how the wind blows! I ain't about to dicker with a bunch of blabbermouthin' fools that can't even keep their business a secret!"

He broke off, seeing that they were both grinning at him. He looked from one to the other, genuinely bewildered. Then the light dawned, and the surprise was even more genuine. He looked searchingly at Toby. "You don't mean she's—"

Toby nodded and inhaled another spoonful of stew. "Hell, we got to git new people sometimes, don't we? The wear and tear on an outfit like ours is apt to be a mite rough once in awhile. Glory, here's, what you might call our recruiter. She's the one that thought you might like to stuff your pants pockets with somethin' besides a few old frazzled-up dollar bills come payday."

Ben sat down and ran a hand over his chin, looking around at the almost deserted restaurant. "It's all right," Glory assured him. "Ma Jenkins is over at the store and Mr. Bassett is—shall we say—sympathetic to our cause? Welcome to the share-the-wealth club, Mr. Johnson."

"Well, fry me for a sucker!" Ben was still shaking his head, and not wholly in pretense. "When you people surprise a man you do it all the way. Maybe I'd ought to meet Mr. Bassett, since we're sort of pardners now."

Toby called Bassett over. Bassett shook hands without apparent reluctance, his eyes now noncommittal. "Welcome, as Glory said," he told Ben in a flat voice. "Hope you like it."

"I like anythin' with money in it," Ben assured him. Something about the hand he was shaking bothered him, then with a start it came to him. *The thumb that was pressed against the back of his hand did not fit the rest of the picture! The other fingers and the palm were soft, as one would expect, but there was a rough ridge of callus on the thumb that actually felt raspy!*

To Ben it spelled one thing, and one thing only. He sneaked a quick look under the pretense of kicking a piece of debris from under his foot, and his suspicions were confirmed. *That* callus was not formed by opening sample cases, or uncorking bottles. It was a gunfighter's thumb, pure and simple, and a callus of those dimensions could only be caused by hard, constant practice. Harlow Bassett took on a new size and shape in Ben's mind.

He was no longer a harmless eccentric in a monkey suit. He could be death masquerading as a jester!

## CHAPTER 16

Ben was now in a real quandary. Toby knew he had already made his call on the sheriff, and if he went back it might well excite suspicion. But this latest development was pure gunpowder, all kegged up with a short fuse.

Harlow Bassett, especially. The man was a complete puzzle, and one that might blow up in a man's face. What was such a ludicrous figure of a man doing with gun-hammer calluses on his right thumb, and if he was good with that gun, what was he doing unheeled?

While Bassett was speaking to Toby, Ben had a chance to study the face more closely. With his experience in reading character, he saw a mixture of cupidity, sullenness, and more than a touch of the spoiled brat. *Put him out on that white-face ranch and he could pass for Charlie Morris' older brother. Put him in a monkey suit like that and he'll want to get out of it. Put him under your thumb—*

Ben's eyes narrowed suddenly as Bassett reached into his inside coatpocket and took out a cigar case. Even before Bassett extracted the long, thin cheroot and reached for a match, something clanged in Ben's mind like a fire bell. So this was the man who talked from the darkness and shot the same way. This was the killer of the little old man who had never done anything meaner in his life than sell some rotgut whisky that people drank at their own risk. It was all Ben could do to keep his big hands off that smooth, talcumed neck.

*And,* this was the man who was suspicious of him, who had approached the old moonshiner in the first place to get him for a spy. That being the case, Ben could well be living on borrowed time, depending on how much Bassett had actually found out.

Ben racked his brain and finally came up with a solution. He *would* get the information to the sheriff, and damn soon! "I'm gonna go git another drink," he announced. "Likely to be danged dry out where I'm a-goin', and I don't aim to start out spittin' cotton."

"Well, make it fast," Toby said grudgingly. "You're s'posed to be on your way right now. Come right back here."

Ben touched the brim of his hat and loped out the door, heading for the Silver Dollar. Inside, as he expected, he found Moss Finley still bending his elbow and glowering around at all and sundry.

The bartender spread his hands with a resigned expression. "Can't do a damn thing with him," he said in a semi-whisper. "Standin' there pawin' the floor and snortin' at everybody that comes in. I won't make enough to pay for my spittoon emptier today. If I wasn't afraid he'd come back and wreck the place, danged if I wouldn't call the sheriff and see if he reely has guts or if he was just eatin' loco weed."

Ben winked at the bartender. "Mebbe you won't need to do that. All ol' Moss needs is a playmate, and I ain't got nothin' better to do."

The bartender was incredulous. "You mean you're goin' to tangle with Moss just for the *fun* of it?"

Ben grinned. "Well, I don't see nobody steppin' up and offerin' me a salary for it, so I reckon you got it straight. Tell you what. Just for a laugh, wait till we git to rollin' in the dirt, and *then* you send someone for good ol' Ace and see if he comes to stop it. Be right interestin' to me, too."

The bartender sighed. "Damned if you fellers don't beat all. Fightin' for fun! Hey now—don't you go startin' it in *here!* I got troubles enough already!"

Ben winked at him, then walked over to Moss, who turned to stare owlishly at him over his newly emptied glass. "Hey!" Moss bellowed. "S'my ol' fightin' pardner, b' God if it ain't! Hey, ol' fightin' pardner! Wanna fight? C'mon, let's you and me take swipes at each another, huh?"

Ben put an arm over Moss's shoulder. "Ol' pal, I come back special on purpose to trade swipes with you. Couldn't bear to go on my way thinkin' of you here pinin' for someone to play with. Ain't no worse fate than for a man to have to go to bed without sore knuckles and a flock of bruises."

"You got it!" Moss roared, pounding the bar. "Here's man that knows livin', I kin tell you! Anyone which says he don't, I'll stomp his liver out!" He bent at the waist, one arm across his middle in an ornate bow, the other log-thick arm sweeping toward the door. "After you, my frien', and if any of these here ribbon clerks bothers you on the way out I'll stomp his dag-nabbed liver out." He stopped, brow wrinkled in a deep frown. "Seems to me like I done said that before. Hell, what's the diff'rence! I'm the best danged stiver stom—the best lipper stiver—" He stopped and glared around the saloon. "Well, anybody says somethin' I'll do it, anyways!" He bowed to Ben again and almost pitched forward on his face.

Ben grabbed him and steadied him on his feet. "C'mon,

ol' fightin' pardner. I'll help you outside and then we'll git down to business."

Moss threw his arms around Ben and burst into tears. "Thass a *real* pal! Tell you what. Let's not you and me fight. Let's you and me fight somebody *else!* Let's fight the whole dang-blasted town!" He pulled back and weaved around the room, his massive fists describing circles in front of him. "C'mon, town, and git your liver stomped out by me and my ol' fightin' pardner! We'll stomp this ol' town's liver so danged flat it'll cover ten acre of ground on the level!" He took a wild swing at the nearest man, who promptly dropped his glass, ducked, and ran. Moss stumbled around kicking over chairs and barking his knuckles on suspicious-looking coat-racks.

Ben finally got him straightened out and headed him for the door. Once outside, Moss reverted to type and all good fellowship was forgotten. He whirled and grabbed Ben in a paralyzing bear-hug that nearly crushed his ribs with the surprise pressure.

Ben's hands were locked in front of him, and he squirmed until he got them together at the pit of Moss's stomach. Then he gripped his hands together with the thumbs sticking out like battering rams. Using Moss's pressure and the full strength of both arms, he brought the thumbs upward and inward in a violent thrust.

Moss's whisky-laden breath whooshed out of him like a hurricane, and the bear-hug relaxed enough for Ben to break loose. He grabbed one thick wrist, whirled until his shoulder was under Moss's armpit, and heaved. Moss left his feet like a bird and sailed ten feet, raising a dust cloud big enough to obscure an elephant.

He got up and shook his head to clear the cobwebs, walling his eyes until he finally was able to sort out Ben from the triplets he had become. Then his teeth bared in a tight grin and he made a weaving rush.

Even then Ben did not hit him, although Moss had his jaw wide open. Instead, he ducked under the roundhouse punch Moss threw and repeated the former process, this time using Moss's momentum to throw him twelve feet.

Moss lay in the dust and roared like a wounded buffalo. "Damn it, pardner, we was s'posed to trade swipes! That's a dirty trick, not tradin' swipes with a feller and gittin' his clothes all dirty! Now I'm a'gonna git up from here and stomp your danged liver out, and if you throw me down here again I'm gonna crawl over and take a bite outta your leg!"

He heaved to his feet and stood for a moment puffing like a wind-broken horse, his face red as a tomato. He raised a forefinger and pointed it at Ben like a pistol. "Now you stand there and wait for me, by grab, and we'll trade swipes, like you promised! I'll be right back. I gotta have another drink to cut this dang dust you been throwin' me in." He made two passes at the swinging doors before he hit them and disappeared inside.

Ace Goodwin must have been watching from his office, and came without being sent for. He did not have the shotgun this time, but his Colt was buckled on. He caught Ben's wink and evaluated it immediately.

"What's goin' on here?" he demanded importantly. Then to Ben, "So! Makin' trouble again, huh? I'd ought to sling you in the pokey and throw the key away!"

Ben scowled. "What the hell's a man s'posed to do when he's picked on all the time? I was just mindin' my own business when that Moss feller—"

Goodwin snorted him down. "I'll *bet!* You ain't minded your own business since you set foot in town."

"That's a damn lie!" Ben howled, and out of the corner of his eye he saw Toby halt in his walk toward them and hunch his shoulders resignedly. "People have been shootin' at me and slingin' fists so damn fast I ain't had time to do nothin' but duck!"

Goodwin hauled out his six-shooter with a flourish. "Call a law officer a liar, will you? All right, Mr. Smart Aleck, you just march ahead of me down to the jail, and if you make one bad move I'll perforate you sure."

Ben grumbled, picked up his old hat, and slammed the dust out of it against his leg. He looked over at Toby and spread his hands helplessly, getting back a black look. Then he went ahead of Goodwin toward the jail.

Once inside, he clapped Goodwin on the back. "Man, you sure missed your callin'! You put on an act that had 'em rollin' in the aisles. Now let's git down to business." He quickly filled the sheriff in on the latest, and when he had finished Goodwin's mouth was hanging open.

"Glory Lambert, of all people, *and that clown!* Ben—I mean Mike—I never been so flabbergasted in my life! You're sure—*real* sure?"

Ben shrugged. "As sure as you can be when somebody tells you right out of their own mouth. She's been their recruiter for Lord knows how long, and he goes around playin' like he's tryin' to peddle that junk of his, and all the time spottin' herds that're easy pickin's."

Goodwin hitched up his pants. "Want me to pick 'em up?"

Ben grinned tightly. "Might be more of a handful than you'd think." He told Goodwin about the gun-hammer callus on Bassett's thumb, and a thoughtful look rearranged the cocky smirk on Goodwin's long face.

"But you said he didn't have a gun when you talked to him?" he asked carefully.

"Nope. *But,* he could go get one, and I got a hunch he might just do that since you picked me up. He strikes me as bein' a pretty cagey customer, so watch out for him. The main thing is we still don't know who the real brains are, so we got to wait till one of them leads us to him. That's where you come in. Pick out somebody you can trust, somebody *not* on your force, and have Bassett watched day and night. Glory, too."

A sneaky look came to Goodwin's face. "Now, *that's* a job I wouldn't want to turn over to anyone else—watchin' *her* day and *night!* All right—all right! So I'm an old goat, but I don't give a dang. That's a right purty bundle of gal."

"A double-barreled derringer's a pretty thing, too," Ben reminded him, "and just about as deadly. Don't forget she had Moss Finley beatin' the be-jeesus out of half the men in the territory just so she could watch. Blood is what she likes, and I got a hunch she'd about as soon see yours as anybody's."

Goodwin shuddered visibly. "You got the dangdest way of spoilin' a feller's daydreams. Reckon you're right, though. Purty or not, she's too dangerous to fool with."

"Make me out a receipt for a hundred dollars," Ben said, and when Goodwin looked at him in bewilderment, went on with impatience, "My fine, damn it! I done talked you out of lockin' me up, but I had to pay the fine now or wait till the judge came around. And don't forget to brag around how you got me for disturbin' the peace."

Goodwin quickly wrote out a receipt and Ben handed him the amount. "That's to wave around while you're tellin' about it. Don't leave nothin' to chance. Now I gotta git. And you have them men up on that hill—one at all times from now on, you hear?"

On the way back to the restaurant, Ben held his breath

until he was a turkey-gobbler red in the face, and when he entered the place he looked like a man on the verge of apoplexy. "That stinkin', money-grabbin', tinhorn excuse for the law!" he exploded when the door closed behind him. "To keep from gettin' locked up till the judge comes around, I had to pony up a hundred hard-earned bucks!" He turned to Toby, his mouth set angrily. "I let you talk me out of stoppin' his clock this time, but when I git to town again—"

"Any other time'll be the same as now," Glory said curtly. *"None* of us would last long if *any* of us went around shooting sheriffs. Do as Toby told you. If you can't seem to get along with Ace Goodwin, stay away from him and don't give him any excuse for getting on you."

Ben yanked off his hat and slammed it against his leg, then drew a deep breath and put it back on his head. "All right now," he said, allowing a trace of a grin to show. "It's just that he gits under my skin like a damn chigger and won't let go. Reckon I might find another town to do my howlin' in when I git some time off."

Toby clapped him on the back. "Now that's playin' it smart! There's plenty of other towns, and they all sell booze if that's what a man's after."

Harlow Bassett dropped the butt of a cheroot on the floor and ground it out with his heel. "What else did the sheriff have to say?" he asked.

Ben turned to him. "You talkin' to me?"

Bassett waited a moment, then nodded slowly. "You're the only one that's been talking to him, so I'd hardly be speaking to anyone else."

Ben's eyes sparked into the cold ones looking at him. "If he'd said anythin' I thought you ought to know, I'd of told you. You got some reason for thinkin' he did?"

Bassett shrugged. "Who knows what a sheriff might talk about? Price of beef—chance of reelection—who killed Cock Robin? . . ."

Ben took two steps to tower over him. *"You* tell *me* little man. Who did kill him, with what caliber bow and arrer?"

Bassett did not flinch, but looked up into the agate-hard eyes. "Or maybe you were talking about the high price of whisky, which the sheriff claims he can't afford on his salary."

Ben sensed the by-play Bassett was handing him, and

failed to rise to the bait. Instead, he turned to Toby. "If I have to be around this feller much, you kin call the whole thing off. I don't mind a body comin' right out and sayin' he don't like me, but I don't like bein' pecked at." He turned again to look at Bassett, watching the man keenly as he spoke. "If you was a western man, and packed a gun, mebbe you wouldn't be so free with your mouth."

Ben did not miss the sudden glint that came into the cold eyes, nor the suggestion of a retort that died as suddenly as it was begun. So Bassett *was* saving something back . . .

It was Toby who saved the situation by stepping between the two, shaking his head at both. "There'll be no fightin' among ourselves. Like you said, Mike, men that don't go armed are apt to run off at the mouth too much. You, Bassett, keep your mouth shut if you can't keep the fish hooks off of your tongue. Mike, you better get goin'. If you ain't to the Slot by midafternoon somebody'll be wonderin' why."

"Well, all right," Ben grumbled, "but things had better be as good as you say, or I'll still take that trip over the hill. I've had plenty of promises before and not a damn one of them ever give me anythin' but more patches on the seat of my pants."

Glory Lambert smiled. "Your patch-seat days are over, Mike. All you have to do is stick with us and play square, and use that gun if you're told to."

Ben grinned. *"Now* you're talkin' my language. If a man's got somethin' to sell, a buyer will look him up, I always say. You might as well know I kin do as good a sellin' job with a Winchester as a hogleg."

"Fair enough," Toby said. "Don't forget your directions, and in case you forgot to remember, you never did get them pants you was gonna buy."

"Shirt, either," Ben said. "Reckon I got time to get them now?"

Toby hunched his shoulders. "All right, but for God's sake make that your last stop! Glory, pour me a cup o' coffee. Mornin's like this plumb ruin me."

Ben walked down the street to the general store and turned in without looking behind, in front, or to either side of the street. Inside, he blinked to accustom his eyes to the change from bright light to dim, and nearly swallowed his Adam's apple when the familiar voice came from the indistinct figure behind the counter. "Howdy, stranger. Can I help you?"

Ben quick-stepped forward to lean over the counter, staring at the man of medium stature wearing the regalia of a store clerk, long black cuffs, and all.

Ben looked at his superior in stupefied amazement. Marshal Ed Hooker, late of Abilene, grinned at him under a respectable brush pile of newly-grown mustache. "Hi, Ben," he said. "Didn't think I was going to let you have all the fun, did you?"

## CHAPTER 17

Ben finally recovered enough to reach over and grab Hooker's hand. "Things're promisin' to git a mite hot around here," he told him. When Hooker nodded, he asked, "How long you been here?"

"Three days. I spent a couple of days out at the land camp with the boys. They're ready to move at an hour's notice. Give me a quick layout."

Ben outlined the situation while he was trying on the longest-sleeved shirt in the store. The sleeves hit him two inches above the wrist joint, but he kept it on. A new pair of Levi's replaced the old, comfortable pants, but Ben kept on the disreputable hat. "Makes good winder dressin'," he told Hooker with a grin. "You got the picture now?"

Hooker nodded. "Reckon you're wondering why Sheriff Goodwin didn't tell you I was here."

"Sort of, but I reckon there's a reason."

Hooker took Ben's money and made change expertly. "Best reason in the world," he said. "He don't know it either."

Ben grunted. "Then how did *you* expect to find out anythin'? You didn't look me up, either."

"Got a little to go on that you didn't know about. Found out after you left that a certain man named Bassett was locating himself out around here pretty permanently. Eastern man, originally; lived in St. Louis for years. Mixed up in a lot of fast deals, some of them with murder involved. Wondered what the attraction was for a man like him. You just cleared it up for me. This girl—never heard of her before, but she probably has some sort of a record, too."

"Wouldn't surprise me. Well, I got to git goin'. Toby'll be havin' kittens. You'll be comin' in with the boys?"

"Couldn't keep me out. Luck."

Ben nodded and headed for the door. Halfway there, he stopped to grin over his shoulder. "Always suspected you was some sort of a ribbon clerk," he drawled, then dodged a thrown boot. . . .

Within a few more minutes, Ben was on his way out of town. He kept watching behind him, but nobody seemed to be following him. The big horse took the road easily, his running walk eating up the miles. When they left the dusty strip at the old blasted oak, he was as fresh as when they started.

Ben stopped several times on the highest points of travel to look back, trying to orient himself with the highest spot between him and town. He finally settled on a sharp peak with a cluster of pines near its top, and deduced that this was the place where Goodwin would station the men.

At any other time, Ben would have just oozed along, enjoying the wonders of nature, but now he kept the big bay clipping it off. As it did many times, the thought of Frank Chambers and his men invaded his mind and darkened any ray of pity he might feel for any of the gang, Toby included. Tarred with the same brush, all of them, and all fit for the same rope. At the same time, Ben felt like he was walking into a lion's den with his eyes shut and his hands tied behind him.

Rumor had it that there were at least fifty men in there, with the possibility of many more. Chambers and his ten men had been hopelessly outclassed from the start.

Ben was riding down a slight dip in the trail when the voice came from up ahead. "That's the place right there, mister. Squat that horse and sing out your name."

Ben stopped the bay and kept his hands well away from his saddle gun and Colts. "Mike Johnson. Reckon you must be either Slim Parker or Gilly Gahagan."

A man with a rifle slid down from a steep rock face. "Gahagan it is, me bucko, and I couldn't have missed guessin' who you are, by the size of you." He cradled the Winchester in the crook of his arm and jerked his head in the direction Ben had been going. "Keep right on. Me own animal's around the bend, and I'll get him on me way by. Toby didn't come?"

Ben shook his head. "Was he s'posed to?"

"Not specially. Only, *he* usually escorts the new ones in

himself. He must have a lot of confidence in you, bucko."

"That suits me," Ben said, and meant it fervently. Had Toby been along, his chances of doing any good and then getting back alive would have been reduced by a great margin. He might as well have stayed in the town.

They passed through the Slot and on into the widening canyon beyond it, and Ben felt as though a door had closed behind him—and, in a sense, it had. According to Toby, the Slot was guarded day and night, and that meant a man would have to clear himself a path back the way he had come. Ben had closely scanned the Slot from both its ends, and it was guarded by high rock ramparts on all sides. A man trying to scale its impossible sides would be picked off like a sitting duck by the guard. It was fight your way through, and it would be plenty tough when you couldn't see anyone to fight.

Gahagan hit the trail hard, and when they stopped for the night Ben estimated they had come at least fifteen miles, all of it in fairly rough going. Supper was a canned bean, cold bacon, hot coffee affair, and little time was wasted afterward before turning in. Gahagan showed no inclination to be watchful, and Ben was pretty well convinced he had been accepted without reservation. With his usual fatalistic acceptance of circumstances, he fell asleep the moment he relaxed his mind, and knew no more until Gahagan rousted him out at daybreak. . . .

It was more of a village than a rustlers' camp. Cabins were strung for half a mile up and down the creek that ran through the narrow canyon, and midway of the row was a cluster of larger buildings that proved to be a well-patronized saloon, a ramshackle hotel, and a store. Ben shook his head in amazement while Gahagan grinned at him.

"Wonderin' where the goods comes from for the store and saloon, I'll wager," the Irishman said. "Well, cows are not the sole aim of the Black Butte bunch, me bucko. Places where the railroad don't go, there's a lot of freight wagons haulin' this and that. Some of the this and that never get where it's supposed to. Winds up here, wagons and all."

They passed a small, strongly constructed building, and Ben had more than a slight start when he saw the bars at the one visible window.

Gahagan jerked a thumb toward the building. "Even got

a jail, as you'll notice. It don't have many patrons, since the laws here are not very strict, but it comes in handy for storing fragile merchandise." At Ben's blank stare, he chuckled. "Got one in there now that's precious as jewels. If ever we are attacked in force and things look bad, our piece of merchandise in there will buy us time and distance."

"Must be a man," Ben hazarded a guess.

"Head of the class for you, bucko. A badge-toter, for the Association, no less. He had the colossal foolishness to come in here with a handful of men to wipe out the nest."

"And you wiped them out instead."

Gahagan nodded. "All but Mister Chambers, who now languishes in yonder durance vile. He's our insurance against disaster, and we treat him with lovin' care."

Ben's mind was racing. This *did* complicate matters. He felt a surge of thankfulness that his friend was alive, but a man penned up in a jail was little more than that. How he could help Frank was another matter, one that would demand a lot of thought. It was no longer a matter of looking over the layout of the rustlers' stronghold and then getting out to lead an attack.

Now he was faced with getting Chambers out with him, and that could prove to be a major undertaking. It was a cinch he was guarded, since he was so precious to the rustlers, and the guard would have to be taken care of first. That part would not be so tough, but there remained the problem of getting a horse and weapons for Chambers.

All during the ride, Ben's mind had been cataloging the route taken, and he knew he could backtrack without too much trouble. He knew from talking to Gahagan that there were guards strung along at intervals so they could signal by gunshots if the Slot was attacked, and they would either have to be by-passed or taken out of circulation. If he had Frank Chambers with him, this would be easier, since they could split up and take any guard from two sides. Any gunshots would alert the others, of course, but that would have to be risked. The main thing was to get out far enough to send his smoke signal and then make a final break for it.

Gahagan took him to a group of bunkhouses and installed him in one. Ben was amazed at the seemingly complete lack of suspicion on the part of the men, finding instead an impersonal disinterest. Apparently the rustlers had been safe in their stronghold for so long that they were immune to any fear of being attacked or even spied on.

After settling his gear on the bunk, Ben strolled down to the saloon, passing the jail on his way. Through the open door to the office, if it could be flattered with that name, he could see a bored-looking guard slouched back in a chair with his spurred boots up on a scarred desk, his hat tilted down over his eyes. He barely looked up when Ben stopped in the doorway.

"New man," Ben said genially, purposely raising his voice. "Name's Mike Johnson."

The guard waved a languid hand toward a decrepit chair. "Johnsons is a dime a dozen in here. So's the Smiths and the Joneses. I'm a Brown, myself. Set."

Ben sat down and began to make a cigarette. "Just rode in with Gahagan. Reg'lar danged town you got here."

Back in the jail, Ben heard the shuffle of feet and was sure Chambers had recognized his voice. "Whatcha got in there, a galliwampus?" he asked.

Brown yawned. "Sort of. Somebody says watch him, so I watch him. Gets damn tedious, too, settin' here watchin' a feller that ain't goin' nowhere anyway."

"Does seem like wasted manpower," Ben agreed. "Them bars on the windows look strong enough to pen a grizzly, and I reckon your inside bars is just as good."

"Sure they are," Brown said with an injured air, "but you try and tell *them* that. Watch him, they say, as if he was gonna chaw his way through them bars and come sashayin' out."

Ben leaned back and blew a cloud of smoke at the ceiling. "Seems like a terrible waste of good drinkin' time, I'd say. Never was in a jail in my life where they watched a feller *all* the time. You mean to tell me they watch this gink around the clock?"

The guard scored a near miss on a battered spittoon with a jet of tobacco juice. "They *think* they do, but it ain't always so. Sometimes a feller's throat gits so danged dry he'd sell his soul for a cold beer, and that's when watchfulness goes out the winder. Oh, none of us leave for *very* long, but them big people'd git plenty sore if they knowed we left at *all."*

He stopped and gazed long and thoughtfully at Ben. "Hope you ain't one of them tattletales that goes and tells teacher who put the mouse in her desk. You look like a purty good feller, and I'd hate like hell to have to plug a man for such a picayune thing."

Ben grinned. "Never told a tale in my life, in school or out. I'm with you. Danged if I kin see how it renders any more tallow to watch that feller all the time."

The guard grunted and slung his feet down off the desk. "Nice to hear you say that. How'd you like to kind of keep your eye peeled on him for awhile so's I kin go wet my whistle? Ain't nobody around here that's goin' to mind—least of all *him.*"

Ben waved a hand. "Brother, go lap up some suds and don't hurry back. I've been settin' my hoss for so long it'll feel like heaven to rear back and put my feet up for a while. Just so's you git back in time for me to hit the grub pile."

"Will do." The guard took one short look around, hitched up his pants, and slouched out the door. He stopped outside and stuck his head back in. "Hey—what'd you say your name is?"

"Mike Johnson."

The guard's face took on a reflective look. "That's what I thought you said, after thinkin' it over. Seems like I heard Toby speak about you. Uh—just forgit what I said about pluggin' you, will you?"

Ben nodded solemnly and watched the lanky figure slouch down the walk. He watched him until he turned in at the saloon, and only then did he come to his feet in a catlike motion. *God, how did it come to be so easy? Handed the layout of the jail on a silver platter!*

He spun on his heel and headed for the rear of the jail.

## CHAPTER 18

Frank Chambers had a broad grin on his stubbled face when Ben stopped outside the barred cell gate. Chambers was in surprisingly good shape for a man who had been penned up for so long. He was a bit on the short side, but with thick, heavy shoulders that spelled power.

"Might know you'd figure out some way to bust into the place," he said, gripping Ben's hand through the bars.

"You're just danged lucky I was brought by here by a talkative Irishman," Ben told him. "Otherwise, I might never have knowed you were here. How you been treated?"

Chambers shrugged. "Good as could be expected. I'm pretty important to them, I reckon, so they've taken care of me like I was a prize hog. Good enough grub—even a beer now and again when one of them thinks to bring one back."

"All right." Ben swiftly outlined what had been done and what was still to be accomplished. "How are them bars?"

Chambers grinned crookedly. "Like the Rock of Gibraltar. Might not need to fool with them, though, if you can bamboozle one of the guards with a bottle."

"Any special one?"

Chambers nodded. "Durango Smith. He's one of the redheaded Smiths—got all kinds here, like Brown said. He's usually on duty after midnight, and that would be the best time anyway. He's a good bottle man—fights it to beat hell. Many a time I've heard the morning guard cussing him when he woke him up."

"Durango's my man, then. And I can tell you it's gonna be just as quick as I can make it—mebbe tonight. What time does he start?"

"Midnight, usually. If he's not already drunk, that is. Then they send over somebody else."

"Keep your fingers crossed for Durango. I better be gittin' back to the office before Mister Brown comes back. Frank, I can't tell you how deep down I'm glad to see you."

Chambers took a deep breath and grinned. "However glad *you* are, you can double it for me. Man, I could have rotted here for the next ten years! Scat!"

Ben looked back at his friend. "Mebbe we're both bein' a mite too sure, *amigo*. This thing *might* go sour."

"Then she's sour," Chambers said, unperturbed. "I'd a hell of a sight rather take my chances out there in the hills with a handful of rocks than look at these bars another day."

Ben was sitting and smoking when Brown came back. He got up and stretched. "My turn now, I reckon. They got anythin' but rotgut in this place?"

Brown grunted as he dropped back into the desk chair. He belched loudly, then said, "They got just about any kind of popskull you got the money to pay for. Some of them freight shipments they grab are dang near all whisky.

All in all, I reckon there's about as much booze freighted into this part of the Territory as there is grub."

Ben got a quick drink in the saloon and then wandered around the settlement looking over the lay of the land. He memorized the positions of the buildings, the back alleys, and footpaths, and most of all he imprinted on his mind how the main street ran to the edge of town, took a turn, and petered out into the trail he had come in on.

Curiosity made him backtrack on the street until it went out the other side of town, and from a slight rise he could see it stretching out into the distance as far as his eyes could reach.

So this was the way they got their freight wagons and other vehicles into the stronghold. And Lord only knew where it came out into the open country. Some well-hidden spot, no doubt, and guarded as jealously as the mint. Also, it would provide a fast getaway route for the gang if they smelled defeat. One way or another, it would have to be plugged before the whole bunch could be taken. That would come later. The job right now was to get Chambers away and signal for the posse to go into action.

The next thing was to plan their own getaway. Ben sauntered around until he found a pole corral full of horses, many of them choice horseflesh. No wonder, Ben thought wryly. A rustler didn't have to buy his mount. All he had to do was to pick it out and steal it. Well, someone would find his horse stolen back from him before morning.

He kept to himself as much as possible, not wanting to create any good fellowship that might be hard to break when he wanted to get down to serious business. Thank the Lord there would be a nearly full moon to light things till dawn. It would be hell trying to negotiate the strange trail without it. A man would be more of a target, of course, but with light he could make it a faster-moving one. . . .

After supper, Ben loafed around the bunkhouse, reading old newspapers, watching poker games, and looking over the hard-bitten crew. He saw the real dregs of the cow country and places beyond, men who had been immersed in crime so long they had nothing to lose and lived that way. Money flowed over the tables like water, as though the players were eager to get rid of it. Easy come, easy go, seemed to be the attitude, although Ben could not for the life of him see how the hard work and risks of cattle rustling could possibly be classed as an easy money game.

Dark came at last, and many of the men left the bunkhouse for the more exciting atmosphere of the saloon. Some of the others, their old cowboy training so ingrained they could not or would not break it, shucked off their outer clothes and went to bed with the chickens. Others sat around reading until the idea for sleep should strike them.

Ben sat with them, occasionally replying shortly to one remark or other directed at him, but purposely staying out of any serious discussions that might involve him to the point of exciting suspicion when he had to break away. About nine-thirty he did just that, arising and stretching and saying he guessed he'd run down to the saloon for a few snifters. Nobody offered to accompany him, happily.

He went into the saloon and bought a quart bottle, taking it to a table with him, purposely sitting in the darkest corner. He drank sparingly, sipping like a bird as he watched the activities going on around him.

Had he not known he was in the middle of the desolate stretch known as the Black Buttes, he could have sworn he was drinking in some prosperous, ordinary cowtown. The dancing girls were even prettier, the furnishings of the establishment were as ornate as the best, and the choice of whisky, as Brown had said, was limited only by a man's ability to pay.

Strangely, he heard less arguing and saw less outright belligerence than he would have in any town he could name. For this, he was forced into a grudging respect for the brains that ran the gang. Instilling such rigid discipline into a gang of cutthroats took more than ordinary talents for handling men. It needed the respect of those men, and the leader evidently had it. As yet, Ben had seen no one individual in this camp who could qualify for such a rating. And, he told himself grimly, he had no intention of sticking around to find him. Now, it was get Chambers out and then make the biggest damn tracks of his career.

When midnight came, Ben had lowered the level of whisky in his bottle by a scant two inches, and judged the remainder would do the trick. He tucked the bottle under his arm and headed for the jail at a leisurely pace. He entered the office and stared solemnly at the frowzy specimen in the desk chair.

"Whoopee," Ben said in a conversational tone. "Reckon you might be ol' Durango Smith, of the red-headed

Smiths? My frien' Brown, of the brown-headed Browns, done tol' me a ol' he-stud drinkin' man name of Red-headed Smith would be spittin' cotton all over this here office tonight, and I couldn't bear to see that happen, not when me, Mike Johnson of the Johnson-Johnsons, has still got a danged drop in his bottle!" He held out the bottle and peered owlishly at it. "Hah! Just remembered—other bottle sprung a leak and went dry, and I had to buy 'nother one for a bed-pardner."

He thrust the bottle toward Durango, who was already licking his lips. "Frien', wrop them flubbery ol' lips aroun' this and do your gut some good. You look like your fire is danged near out."

Durango reached for the bottle with a trembling hand. "Brother, you never said truer words," he croaked. "If'n you had wings you couldn't be more of a angel right this minute!" He snatched the bottle, held it toward the oil lamp for a moment to tease himself with its amber magic, then leaned back slowly into his chair and opened his mouth like a baby robin waiting for a worm.

Ben sat down and watched in open-mouthed admiration the free-style drinking technique displayed by Durango Smith, of the red-headed Smiths. The bottle said, "Glug," and then settled down to a monotonous repetition of that simple phrase. At every *glug,* Durango's Adam's apple darted up and down like a dog trying to escape from a collapsed tent, and his eyes batted rhythmically, four times to the *glug*.

As the whisky level in the bottle lowered, his skin gradually turned to a violent pink, his huge freckles standing out like brown butterflies. Sweat popped out on his forehead and he wiped it off with his shirtsleeve without missing a swallow. Finally he reluctantly gave up, the *glugs* slowing in tempo and dying to a limpid gurgle as though the bottle were laughing.

Durango's mouth came open and a great "Whoosh" burst out. He gasped for breath and handed back the half-emptied bottle, clawing the air with his free hand. Sweat was pouring off his face in streams.

"Brother," he managed to say at last, "you done saved a life this night! Now I kin face these here lonely hours with a happy gut and stiddy hand. What'd you say your name was?"

"Was and is Johnson—Mike Johnson—and I reckon I better git me a little nibble out of that bottle 'fore I hand it back over to you. You take to a danged bottle like a lost lamb."

Durango was still breathing hard, his nostrils flaring with every breath, but his eyes followed the bottle as Ben gurgled it a few times. When it was handed back he clutched it as though he had never seen it before. "Sure you don't mind?" he asked hopefully.

Ben waved a hand. "Women was made to love, money to spend, and whisky to drink. Have at it, pardner, and if that one gits too big a leak in it I'll go trade some money for another one. I *like* to drink with a man that ain't afraid to fight hell out of the bottle."

Durango seemed to feel it necessary to uphold the fine reputation Ben had invented for him, and in less than ten minutes Ben was on his way for another quart. And within another five minutes he had left the bottle with Durango while he went for a horse he had spotted earlier. Ten minutes after that he was back with his own horse and the appropriated one. He tied them in back of the jail and again went inside.

Durango was weaving even while sitting down, the bottle alternating between nestling in his lap and being raised with both hands to be slobbered over. Ben sat impatiently for another ten minutes while the concentrated doses of alcohol did their work, finally taking the bottle from the limp hands and arranging Durango so that he looked to be asleep with his feet propped up on the desk. Only then did Ben begin a systematic search for the keys to the cells.

He gave up on the desk, finally going to the back. "Any idee where they keep them damn keys?" he asked Chambers.

The answer came swiftly. "In the gun case, I *think*. Take a look, and if they're not there you might have to shoot out this damn lock and bring them all down on us."

Ben went back to the front office, jerked open the door to the closed gun rack, and breathed a sigh of relief. He snatched up the ring of keys and in a few seconds was trying them in the cell door. The third one worked, and Chambers was free. They closed and locked the cell after arranging the blankets on the bunk in a rude dummy form.

"Horses out back," Ben said. "I'll go take a look first. When I tap on the wall with my gun, slide out easy and come around the south side."

He strolled through the office and out the door, stopping on the walk to roll a cigarette. He looked in both directions, seeing nothing but one man weaving out of the saloon and turning the other direction. He drifted to his left, turning the corner of the building into the shadows cast by the moon. He cat-footed to the rear, seeing that the horses were still undisturbed before he returned.

A second thought struck him, and he reentered the office. From the gun case he took two Winchesters and stuffed four boxes of shells into his jacket pockets, then again went outside. A few seconds later he tapped on the wall, and Chambers joined him. "Like taking candy from a baby," Chambers whispered as they mounted.

"We *hope,*" Ben answered. "This is the easy part. Let's go."

He handed two boxes of shells and one of the rifles to Chambers, who cradled the gun lovingly in his hands. While they rode down the dark alley the released prisoner stuffed cartridges through the loading slot of the weapon until it was full. "Now I feel like a whole man again," he told Ben, who was loading his own rifle.

Ben reached into his saddlebag and handed Chambers a sixgun. "Mebbe this'll help even more. Borryed it from one of the boys that was already asleep when I left. Reckon he won't miss it before mornin'."

They rode slowly down the alley, then diagonally on a footpath after the buildings ended. After perhaps a hundred yards the path converged with the trail out of the south end of the settlement, and Ben heaved a sigh of relief when they were swallowed up by the first shadowy bend without having been challenged.

"Sorry I wasn't able to steal any grub," he told Frank Chambers, "but I didn't want to take a chance. Reckon we can go with empty bellies for a day if we have to. All I've got is some hardtack I always carry in my bags."

Chambers laughed. "Man, I'll live on this free air! Nothing in this world ever smelled so good."

"How's that horse I picked out for you?"

"Feels good. I see you've still got the same old plow horse."

Ben grunted. "This animal will pack me all day and still show his heels to the ones carryin' shrimps like you. Well, this calls for a mite of speed, so we'll trot them for a couple of minutes, then walk for the same time. Feel like you can make it?"

"I'll make it. Set your pace."

All through the night they pressed on. Chambers, his muscles softened by months of imprisonment, suffered in silence as the jolts of his trotting horse hammered at his spine and buttocks. Ben kept asking if he wanted to rest, getting nothing in return but a tight-lipped, "*No!*"

The eastern sky was turning gray when Chambers finally consented to a short blow. They turned off the trail into a small side canyon where a little stream trickled, loosening the cinches to let the horses get a complete rest.

Chambers got down stiffly when they stopped, a tight grin on his drawn face. "You might have to lift me back on here if I stiffen up any more, but it's going to feel good to get my feet on the ground again. Break out some of that hardtack. Might not go too bad with branch water."

After they had eaten, Ben climbed the nearest knoll to look around and get his bearings. Off to the south he could see the peak that Goodwin would probably have his men stationed on. His own position, however, was not quite high enough for his purpose, and he went back to Chambers.

"Gotta make some medicine purty quick," he told him, "soon's I find me a high hill."

Chambers grinned. "Still using that old hilltop telegraph of yours, huh?"

"Know anythin' better?" Ben challenged. "Man can see a smoke column far as his eye'll reach, and as long as he can read what he's seein' it can't be beat. Plenty Injuns runnin' loose that *wouldn't* be if they didn't have signals."

Chambers nodded. "Just joshing you. Where do you figure on making your medicine?"

"*First* high hill, brother. We've been lucky as a couple of corncrib rats, but God knows how long it's goin' to last. The trail guards must've all been asleep when we come through, but you can bet the one—if there *is* only one at the Slot—*won't* be asleep."

Chambers nodded thoughtfully. "You say your boss was going to have the men within a mile of the trail at daybreak this morning?"

Ben grinned. "Just waitin' for my medicine. He was goin' to bring 'em over in boxcars last night from Woodbury. You remember Jim Manley. He's in charge of them. They'll be somewhere close to where the trail leaves the road. Manley, he'll be on some high place, too, tryin to see my smoke so's he won't have to wait for the other fellers to bring him the message."

"Reckon he'll have somebody scouting the trail into the Slot?"

"Likely. Them fellers don't leave much to chance. Once we git to the Slot, if anythin' starts we can count on help before long."

Chambers arose painfully and tightened the cinch on his horse. "Better be on our way. Getting pretty light."

They mounted and wheeled their horses toward the mouth of the little canyon, then reined them to a stop. "Yep," Ben said softly. "The luck done run out."

Facing them, drawn up in a silent line, were four riders, and even in the dim light Ben could see that one of them was—Toby. . . .

## CHAPTER 19

It was even more of a shock to Ben to see that Toby was flanked on his left by Charlie Morris, the spoiled brat. The other two were strangers, but both looked like salty customers. As yet none had drawn a gun, evidently counting on their superior force to provide the balance of power.

"Hello, Toby," Ben said quietly. "Sorry it had to be you. Can't say the same for your left-hand man, there."

"You don't need to say anything for me," Charlie said with a glower. "You'd better say a lot for yourself—and fast. Not that it'll do you any good."

"I see you turned our bird loose," Toby said. "That why you wanted in there, Mike?"

Ben shook his head. "Never even knowed he was there. Turns out your bird's an old friend of mine, and I thank you for keepin' him healthy and full-feathered for me. Another thing, Toby—name's Stratton—Ben Stratton."

There was a swift, audible intake of breath from the man on Toby's right, and his hand jerked visibly. *"Poison, Toby!"* he muttered. "If we're gonna take him, we all gotta go at once."

"I seen three that tried that, just awhile back," Toby said quietly. Then to Ben, "You oughtn't to make people like you, Mister Stratton. It's damn hard to try to kill a man you like, even when he's on the other side of the fence."

Ben nodded. "I know. Same goes here, but I don't reckon it makes much difference. We each got a job to do, and if we git in each other's way somebody's got to climb over. Ol' Charlie there had me guessin' for awhile. You done a purty good job of keepin' him covered up."

Toby shrugged. "Takes a lot of money to keep a man like Charlie in women and whisky—he's got *taste*. Don't git the idee he's a friend of mine—he ain't. He's just handy."

"Sorry we can't stay and chew the fat, Toby, but I got a meetin' to keep outside of the Slot. You figger on makin' me miss it?" Then low to Chambers, "Start from the right."

"Reckon," Toby said, and went for his gun.

Ben threw himself sideways off his horse, seeing from the corner of his eye the blur of Chambers' arm as he flicked the borrowed sixgun out of his waistband. Then his own gun was out and thundering before he hit the ground, doubling the man on Toby's right into a deep bow. His had been the first gun clearing leather, and Ben's quick eye had seen where the greatest danger lay.

Ben rolled like a cat, head always to the attackers, flicking off shots at every roll, until he felt himself drop into the shallow depression he was headed for. A couple of loose head-sized rocks gave a minimum of shelter, and he hugged the ground while he steadied his aim and blasted the other stranger. Charlie Morris was wandering in a tight circle like a chicken that had not quite been decapitated, his head canted oddly over on his right shoulder, his emptied gun clicking impotently as his thumb and forefinger still unconsciously kept up their partnership.

Ben had been counting automatically, and knew he had but one shot left. He and Chambers had loaded their guns to the full six-shot capacity for just such emergencies. Otherwise, he would now be out of bullets.

Toby was crouched low and weaving, but apparently unhurt, and it was with deep, genuine regret that Ben sent that last shot crashing into him. Toby fell like a rag doll, his gun arching from his hand to land in a puff of dust several feet away.

"Frank!" Ben called without taking his eyes from the slowly sinking Charlie and the others. "How you doin'?"

"Hit, but not bad," came the answer, and only then did Ben look toward the voice. Frank's horse was down and he was crouched behind it, now aiming the rifle he had jerked from the saddle boot.

Ben got up cautiously and made his way to the downed gunmen. As he approached, Charlie finally ran down and pitched heavily forward on his face. Toby stirred and rolled slightly, and Ben went to kneel beside him.

The young face was ashen and blood was running from the lower corner of his mouth, but the devil-may-care grin was still trying to take over. "So it wasn't no fluke when you got them other three," he whispered. "Thought mebbe my luck might hold."

Ben raised his head and put both their hats under it. "Man makes his own luck," he told the dying man. "You could just as easy be doin' this for me. Hell of a time to preach, but I wish to hell you'd stayed on the other side of the fence."

"No—regrets," Toby gasped. "I done counted up my chances before I clumb over. Didn't count on you, though. Thought I'd found us a winner." Then the grin broke through. "Reckon I did, at that, but for the wrong side. How's ol' Charlie?"

Ben took a brief glance. "His women and whisky habit is broke."

"Poor ol' Charlie. No more women and whisky—the *tasty* kind. No more—no more . . ."

Toby's head rolled sideways and his breathing ceased, a derisive half-smile still on his face.

Ben put Toby's hat over his face and wiped off his own with a handful of grass before he put it on. He walked over to see how Chambers was doing. He found him tying a neckerchief tightly around his upper left arm with his teeth and the other hand.

"Let me do that," Ben said, and saw Chambers looking oddly at his left side.

"Hope you've got an extra shirt," Chambers commented. "Somebody sure ruined that one."

Ben explored with his fingers, and only then did he feel the hot smart of a bullet furrow across his short ribs. His shirt, where it fit tightly across his middle, had been slit by a bullet as neatly as though it had been done with a pair of shears. There was a seepage of blood sogging his pants and drawers.

"Damn!" he grumbled. "My new clothes, too!" He helped Chambers rough-dress his wound, then turned his attention to his own. He found a clean handkerchief in

Charlie's pocket and padded the crease with it, binding it in place with his old shirt, which he took out of the saddlebag.

The horses of the other men, which they had abandoned when the shooting started, had scattered into the brush, and Ben rounded up one for Chambers. They reloaded all weapons and sent their animals at a dead run down the canyon trail. A half-mile further on Ben suddenly raised a hand. There was a dim side trail turning off up a high hill, and he turned his horse on it.

"Find yourself some thick bushes and *stay in them!*" he called to Chambers, then sent the big bay plunging up through the overhanging brush. Thorns and stiff branches tore at his clothes and finished the ruining job the gunman's bullet had started on his shirt.

He came to the summit and was relieved to see that the hill overlooked everything between there and the Slot. He jumped down and began gathering brush, piling it in an open spot. He scooped up a handful of dry leaves and twigs, shoving them under the greener stuff, and touched a match to it.

In less than a minute the pile had caught, and Ben was back from his horse with a blanket from his bedroll. Waiting until the rising smoke column grew thick and dark, he flipped the blanket over the top of the pile, then off again several times to make distinct, separate puffs.

He repeated the procedure several times, each series different in the number of puffs, then kicked the pile of burning brush into a scattered mess. In a few seconds he was again on his horse, plunging back down the dim trail.

Chambers was waiting for him, and once more they continued on toward the Slot. This time they rode more slowly, and Ben got off to reconnoiter each turn in the trail before they rode around it.

"Wonder how Toby got onto me," Ben said to Chambers. "Should have had sense enough to ask him, but he prob'ly wouldn't have told me anyhow. Keep your eye out behind, Frank. Them guards strung along sure ain't asleep *now. . . .*"

Outside the Slot, Marshal Hooker, now dressed in range clothes since his masquerade as a store clerk was over, beckoned Jim Manley to him. "Get what he said with that smoke?"

The hard-faced, flinty-eyed Manley nodded. "Sent five

big puffs the first time. Meant no big force followin' him. Next three meant there was still guards somewhere around that gap up yonder. My men got two spotted already. Last two puffs meant hit it fast and hard, and he'd take 'em from the other side."

Ace Goodwin edged into the gathering that formed around Hooker. "How'll you know you're shootin' at them guards and not Stratton?"

Hooker grinned. "He'll let us know, don't you worry. He's got a voice like a wounded buffalo when he wants to use it, and he'll *use* it. Ready, Manley?"

Manley nodded and whistled sharply. Immediately, from a quarter-mile ahead, rifles cracked as the advance scouts opened fire on the hidden guards. Answering fire showed that resistance was still to be expected.

Manley strode to the brow of the knoll, his heavily armed men massed on the flat below. He swept up an arm, and as one man the hard-bitten crew swung into their saddles. At once Manley mounted and rode down to head them. Hooker and Goodwin caught up their own horses and mounted, but already the column was strung out along the trail, compelling them to fall in where they could.

When they got close to the sound of firing, Manley raised a hand and the column stopped. Without an order given, thirty men dragged their rifles from the boots, slid off their horses, and glided into the brush rimming the trail. As parts of a well-oiled machine, others rode forward and took the reins of the abandoned horses, leading them off the trail for others to retrieve at the end of the column, where they would again be available for their riders.

"God!" Goodwin gasped to Hooker. "I thought I'd seen some tough hombres in my day, but these is absolutely frightenin'! Glad *I* ain't up there tryin' to hold that gap agin' em."

In less than a minute a fusillade began up ahead, lasting for perhaps ten seconds. Then they saw a figure appear on a prominence and wave an arm, and once again the column was on the move.

"If I'd of had these men long ago," Goodwin was muttering. "If only I'd of had these men long ago I'd of cleaned out that nest like a b'ar empties a calf corral."

"Sure you would," Hooker assured him. "Man can't do a job like that without a lot of help."

Goodwin shot him a grateful look, and they rode on

with the column, into the narrowing pass and into the Slot. Then from somewhere up ahead they heard a bull roar.

"Hey, Jim! Jim Manley! Got an old friend of yours here!"

When they arrived at the wide spot past the Slot, they found Frank Chambers shaking hands all around. Hooker took his turn, as did Goodwin. Then without further preliminaries Ben briefed the men, Manley in particular, on what they would find farther on. "You goin' on in?" he asked Hooker.

Hooker nodded. "Might as well see the thing finished. Get off that horse and we'll fix up that wound." One man was already expertly bandaging Frank's shoulder.

Ben grudgingly got down and fidgeted impatiently while the wound was turpentined and bound. He shoved what was left of his shirttail down in his pants.

"You come on back to town with me," he directed Goodwin. "There'll be some formal charges to be made and I'll need you there to take care of it. Marshal, I'll get on the telegraph as soon as I get in and have the sheriff over in Pottsville take a posse over where that road comes out. He likely knows where it is, or close to it." Then he grinned. "Luck, ribbon clerk."

"Go to hell!" Hooker growled, then his lips quirked. "Good job, Ben. Getting Frank out, especially. Sure you won't need some more help in town?"

"What for? Me and the sheriff can handle anythin' we find there." Ben saw from the corner of his eye the slight swell to Goodwin's skinny chest. *At least, the reluctant warrior had come along on one that promised to be tough.*

And at that moment, in the town of Longhorn, a man decided he had waited long enough for recognition and reward, and made his plans accordingly. . . .

## CHAPTER 20

Ben, Frank Chambers, and Goodwin rode into town about two hours later, having pushed their horses in order to get Frank to the doctor as soon as possible. They went in by a back street, not wanting to alert Bassett and Glory Lambert.

Leaving Frank with the doctor, Ben went alone to the

restaurant. There were no customers, and Glory's eyes widened when he came in. She hurried to the counter.

"Mike!" she said in a low voice. "What are you doing back here? You're supposed to be—"

"I know," he interrupted, "but somethin' came up I wanted to talk to Toby about. Is he around?"

To his relief, her answer showed that she had not been told anything, so Toby must have gone to the Slot directly from the ranch after he had found out about Ben's real job. "He didn't come in today. What is it, Mike?"

He kept his voice as low as hers. "Somethin' wrong, is all I can say. When I got to that Slot, I waited and waited, but there wasn't nobody around. I yelled, but nobody showed up. Then I went on through, and I rode the whole afternoon without even bein' challenged, after Toby told me there was guards strung all along the trail. *Somebody,"* he added pointedly, "better hear about this, and fast."

Glory chewed her lip, her eyes on the bloody bandage. "And you're hurt! How did you get that?"

Mike had thought this all out in advance. "If you want my guess, there's some spooky stuff goin' on, and I ain't forgot how that Bassett kept throwin' the hooks into me that day. My idee is he'd like to git out of that monkey suit and be the big man he thinks he is."

There was a swift intake of breath as Glory caught her lower lip between her teeth. "That's got to be it! He's been jealous of my standing, and jealous of—of the boss. He was in here just a little while ago, and I *thought* he was acting funny. He said something about—" Suddenly her face whitened. "Mike! It *has* to be Bassett! More than once he's made remarks about getting the last laugh, and somehow he must have gotten the men to go along with his ideas! When he left here he said he was going to pull off a big deal, but wouldn't say what."

Ben shrugged. "Sounds to me like mebbe he's goin' to make sure of himself by movin' *somebody* out of the way."

"Mike, you've got to stop him! That's what it is, I'm sure! Go after him—*stop him!"*

Ben grinned crookedly. "If I had any idee where I was supposed to go, it might be a little easier."

"The schoolhouse—right here in town! *The schoolteacher, Hugh Andrews, is our boss!* If Bassett kills him and gets complete control of the gang, neither of our lives is worth a plugged nickel!"

Ben headed for the door. "Stick here," he said, and ran for his horse.

He hesitated just long enough at the jail to call Goodwin out and tell him to take Glory into custody, then sent his horse at a run for the schoolhouse.

The schoolhouse was only a couple of streets away, and the big bay ate up the distance in no time. Ben stopped him a short distance away and dismounted. He was bone-tired and his side felt as though it had a hot poker lying across it, but the prospect of a final wrap-up of the case gave him a drive that made all else unimportant.

He walked toward the building, and was still fifty feet from the door when it opened and a small, gray-haired, frightened-looking man emerged. At his back was Bassett, and at sight of Ben the little man squeaked and dove off the small entry porch.

"He's going to kill me!" he cried out, trying to burrow under the porch floor.

Bassett stood with his left side to Ben, his coat making it impossible to determine whether or not he was wearing a gun. "What are you doing here?" he demanded. "You're supposed to be—"

"I know where I'm s'posed to be, and I got a hunch *you* know why I'm not there, Bassett. I'm here to arrest you both for cattle stealing and other crimes, and likely for murder. If you have a gun, throw it down!"

Bassett did not hesitate an instant. Ben had kept edging at a side angle until Bassett was no longer between him and the building, so that any missed shot would not imperil the children in the flimsy building.

With the ease born of long, patient practice, Bassett's hand swept back the coattail and obeyed its hard-won lessons with flawless perfection. The thumb curled over the hammer, cocking it as the gun cleared the holster, and the forefinger slid inside the trigger guard with familiar ease.

*Strange!* For some reason or other he could not raise the gun—was even being driven back on his heels by a violent blow on his chest! Things were not supposed to go this way. It was the big man who should be falling, instead of standing rock-hard with a smoking gun in his hand—a gun that had not been there a split-second before!

Then the numbing shock drove all consciousness from his mind, and Bassett died with his one consuming ambition unfulfilled—that of proving his equality with a gun.

Ben walked over to look down at him. He told one of

the larger boys to dismiss the school, then reached down over the edge of the porch and picked Hugh Andrews up by the back of his coat collar, holding him up with one hand for inspection as though he were some strange bug.

"Little man," he said, disgust making his voice razor-edged, "you've made big trouble, but now you've got it all back. If you ain't practiced up on your prayin', you better git started."

"No, no!" Andrews babbled. "I *can't* stop now—not when I've got almost all I need!" His voice dropped to a pleading tone. "Can't you see? I needed the money to do the things I've always wanted—there was no other way—teachers don't make much money, and—*there was no other way!*"

Then Andrews looked around furtively, his eyes wet and shiny. "It's not too late!" He was whispering now, hoarse and frantic in his desperation. "You and I—we can split what I have and neither of us will be poor again. Look—I'll even trust you. There's a trapdoor under my desk that—"

"Thanks. I'll dig it up later." Ben shoved him toward Goodwin, who had arrived just in time to be too late. "All yours," Ben told Goodwin. "Soon as you git back we'll take a look under that schoolhouse floor. . . ."

Five days had passed. Marshal Hooker and his men had gone through the Black Butte country like a giant broom, sweeping the outlaw stronghold into a broken, burnt-out wreck. The rustlers themselves had been killed or captured almost to a man, the few survivors riding far and away. The big machine was put out of order permanently, it was hoped.

Ben, Hooker, and Goodwin were sitting in the office after winding everything up. Goodwin scowled at Ben. "Saddle tramp!" he growled in disgust.

Ben grinned. "Yep."

"Come in here lookin' like some damned saddle bum, and *actin'* like one. 'Less I miss my guess, you must've been one oncet. Nobody could *act* that good."

"Yep."

Ben tilted his chair back against the wall and started manufacturing a cigarette. "What puzzles me is—" he began, then his fingers stopped moving while his brows knit. He made his voice as casual as possible. "Funny, how things git around. Seems like you can't depend on nobody to keep quiet. That feller must've told Toby first time he seen him that I was a marshal."

He watched narrowly while Goodwin shook his head. "Didn't think Marty was so danged loose-mouthed," Goodwin said. "All I told him was—"

Flakes of tobacco and the cigarette paper cluttered the air as Ben lunged out of his chair and leaned over the desk. He snatched Goodwin by the front of his vest and pulled him up close to scowl into his face.

"You did, did you!" he roared. "You damned fool, Marty and Toby was good friends, and he'd never dream Toby was one of the bunch! Now have you got it through that thick head of yours how you dang near got me and Frank Chambers killed?"

Goodwin's jaw dropped. "My Gawd, Marty must've told him right off, or even Charlie! And then they got them other two hardcases that likely worked at the ranch, and— Hey! What the hell you think you're doin'!"

Ben had picked him up and tucked him under one arm, his long arms and legs flailing. Hooker sat impassively, a slight grin tugging at the corners of his mouth as Ben picked up the ring of keys and headed for the jail section.

"Hey!" Goodwin bawled, thrashing vainly in the iron grip. "You put me down, you hear! Hooker, make this damn maniac put me down! Now you cut that out!"

Ben unlocked the door to Andrews' cell and thrust Goodwin inside, locking the door after him. "Now, you damned fool, sit in there for awhile and scratch and think! And if you and your pardner Mister Andrews git tired of scratchin' yourselves you kin scratch each other."

"You can't do this, dagnab it!" Goodwin howled. "There might not be anybody come in here all day! Both my deputies is out of town!"

"I'll leave the keys on the desk," Ben told him. "You won't be here long enough to starve I *hope.*"

"Mike—I mean Marshal."

Ben turned toward the cell where Glory Lambert was being held for trial. "Ma'am?"

"You're a slick one. You had me even thinking of cozy cottages and kids with runny noses and chickens clucking all over the place. What a way for it to end. But if—maybe it doesn't have to end, if you'd—"

Ben's mouth twisted faintly. "Thanks for the offer, but I don't think I'd hanker for goin' through life drawin' blood for you to see."

Her voice went low—throaty. "Come a little closer. There's something you ought to know that I don't want the others to hear."

Ben took a step closer, then stopped, her spittle running down his face. "I'm glad you done that," he said without anger. "I was nearly feelin' sorry for you, but now I know better."

Hooker was on his feet when Ben returned to the office, and they walked out to their horses. "Finished," Ben said. "Sure will seem nice to just set around for awhile and watch the toes of my boots."

Hooker shook his head regretfully. "Sorry, Ben, but I'm afraid you'll be doing something with those boot toes besides watching them. Still got those old clothes?"

Ben sagged against his horse and moaned in anguish. "Oh, no! Not *again!* Boss, this one just about finished *me!* Shot up, punched, et alive by Goodwin's bugs—spit on—"

"This one might not be so bad. Nothing to it. All you have to do is ride out Arizona and—"

"Ride out?" Ben asked hollowly.

"Well, now, you wouldn't expect a saddle bum to come riding in somewhere on a train, would you? A man that's supposed to be working his way through the grub line—"

"All right—*all right!* What am I gettin' into?"

Hooker swung up on his horse and looked at Ben with an innocent expression. "Why, Benjamin, surely you can handle an argument between two little bitty old towns! You'll find your instructions written out in your saddlebags, and a few other things you might need, like the letter of introduction from a man you used to work for—a big sheep dealer in Chicago."

*"Sheep?"* Ben's roar brought heads from doorways. "You mean to tell me you've gone and tied me in with some kind of a *sheep* deal? Why, you—!"

Then he fell silent and shook his head in resignation. After all, what was the use of talking to a man's back and a horse's swaying rump? Especially when it wouldn't do any good anyway, with them getting farther away all the time. . . .